THE W
OF HO

# THE WAY OF HOLINESS

## A Guide to living with Spiritual Discipline

ROBERT VAN DE WEYER

**Fount**
*An Imprint of* HarperCollins*Publishers*

0006276059

200299909

248.4

First published in Great Britain
in 1992 by Fount Paperbacks

Fount Paperbacks is an imprint of
HarperCollins*Religious*
Part of HarperCollins*Publishers*
77–85 Fulham Palace Road, London W6 8JB

Phototypeset by Intype, London
Printed and bound in Great Britain by
HarperCollins Manufacturing Glasgow

A catalogue record for this book is available
from the British Library

# CONTENTS

# 6 The Way of Holiness

## PART 3 OBEDIENCE

## PART 3  OBEDIENCE

## EPILOGUE                                   195

# INTRODUCTION

For over two millennia monks and nuns of all the great world religions – Judaism, Christianity, Hinduism, Buddhism and Islam – have been seeking perfection. They have tried to create a way of life which is in harmony both with the natural environment and with their own souls and bodies. And to a remarkable extent they have succeeded. As anyone who has visited many monastic communities can testify, there is frequently an atmosphere of peace and serenity, deriving not from some other-worldly escapism, but from the members having wrestled honestly and courageously with all the deepest problems and challenges of human life. And as anyone who has read the history and literature of monasticism can bear witness, monks and nuns throughout the centuries have often possessed a profound and practical wisdom, from which all of us can benefit.

Monasticism has been my own primary guide and inspiration throughout my adult life. Although I am married with children, and have earned my living in the world, I have found myself – often unconsciously – trying to apply the ancient insights of the monks within my own life. And as a priest and counsellor, I frequently encourage others to do the same, with very happy results. This book is simply an attempt to share that wisdom more widely.

The monastic way of life is encapsulated in the three vows which the monk takes: of poverty, chastity and obedience. For the monk poverty means literally owning nothing, chastity means forgoing all sexual relationships, and obedience means accepting without demur the will of the community. Thus on the face of it these vows have no relevance to ordinary married people living in the world. Yet, as monastic writers have always made clear, the vows contain within them far deeper and wider truths that apply to all human beings and to every aspect of life. Poverty defines the right attitude to the whole material environment; chastity defines the right way in which human beings, including husbands and wives, should relate to one another; and obedience defines the relationship between human beings and their Creator. So this book is a commentary on these three vows, as they apply to ordinary people living in the world.

In the past couple of decades two movements, separate yet closely related, have begun to transform moral attitudes within Western society: the 'green' movement, concerned with our relationships with the environment; and the 'holistic' movement, concerned with physical and psychological health. The monasteries were pioneers, centuries before their time, in green and holistic living. Thus monastic literature is a treasure trove of ideas and insights as to how individuals and small groups can adopt a green and holistic way of life. Indeed by following the monastic way many of the follies to which these two movements are prone can be avoided. And, more importantly, green and holistic living can be seen to be both sensible and practical for us all.

The word which monks and nuns traditionally use to describe the monastic way of life is 'holy'. To modern ears this word may sound unduly pious and even priggish. But in fact 'holy' means 'whole' and the fashionable word 'holistic' derives from it. The monastic life is designed to make people whole, both within themselves and in their relationship with the environment. So a person living in the world need feel no embarrassment in saying, 'I want to be holy'. And the simple ideas contained in this book are a modern map of what the prophet Isaiah called 'The Way of Holiness'.

Like the traditional monastic rule, this book is not a continuous narrative, which needs to be read from start to finish. Each chapter within it stands on its own, so you can dip into any topic that especially concerns you. Indeed the order in which the different topics are placed is to some extent arbitrary, encouraging you to take them as you wish. But taken together the thirty chapters do comprise a comprehensive guide to holy living. The great founder of the Jesuits, St Ignatius, required his new recruits to undergo a thirty day retreat, in which they had to reflect critically on every aspect of their lives, to prepare themselves for the rigours of Christian mission. Holiness as described here is far more gentle and earthy than the spiritual athleticism required of the Jesuits. But you may find it helpful, over a period of a month, to read one chapter each day, giving yourself perhaps ten or twenty minutes of silence to reflect on how its contents apply to you. And at the end of each chapter a simple 'task' is suggested, to help put the monastic wisdom into practice. Perhaps your spouse or a group of friends can share this informal 'retreat'; in which case you could meet three times in the course of a month, at the end of each part, to share your reflections.

If at the end you are eager and willing to follow the holy way of poverty, chastity and obedience – and thus be a monk in the world – you shall, in Isaiah's words, be on the 'Way of Holiness'.

# PART 1

*Poverty*

# MONEY

No one should seek any personal advantage from his work.
Everything you do should be for the service of the community.
And you should learn to work with more zeal and enthusiasm
than if you were working for your own profit.

Philip Neri

# MONEY

The first Christian monk, St Anthony, was prompted to give away his property and go out into the desert when he heard the story of the rich young man being read in church. He himself was rich and young, so the words of Jesus, 'Go and sell what you have, and give it to the poor', seemed directed straight at him. And for the following fifty years the hundreds of men that followed Anthony into the desert, in Egypt and Syria, also abandoned all their worldly goods, living in caves and eating whatever wild roots and berries they could find. So the call to poverty was the foundation of monastic life.

Then early in the fourth century St Pachomius began to form monks into communities. They built houses, kitchens, refectories, chapels, and even libraries. Thus by the standards of St Anthony the monks became quite affluent. But everything was owned by the community as a whole, so that the individual monk had no personal wealth. This remained the pattern for about a thousand years.

But in the twelfth and thirteenth centuries new religious orders began to be formed, inspired by men such as St Francis and St Dominic, in which the members wandered from place to place, preaching and teaching. Francis himself owned nothing – but claimed he owned everything, because every living creature was his personal concern. And he and his followers taught that everyone should show the same love and care for the natural world, regarding themselves as stewards of God's creation. Both Francis and Dominic founded religious societies for married people, specifying a simple rule of life for them to follow. This stipulated not only daily prayer and meditation, but also a regular review of stewardship in which members had to discuss with a priest how they used their wealth and their time. Thus the principle of poverty was now being applied directly to men and women in the world.

Over the years these monastic societies for married people have developed the review of stewardship into a fine art. The underlying principle is that all our time and wealth belong to God, to be used according to his will; and thus the priest, with whom individuals and couples discuss stewardship, asks questions and offers advice, to ensure that spiritual and moral considerations are brought to bear on every aspect of daily life. In particular, people should always try to act in accordance with the laws of nature – which are divine laws – so that their actions enhance, rather than destroy, the bounty and beauty of God's creation. Once such an attitude is adopted, then the desire to accumulate wealth melts away, since, like St Francis, people regard the whole world as their own, to be both enjoyed and cherished.

In the modern economy we have come to regard money as the main yardstick for measuring our wealth and our use of time. We value our work according to the money we can earn; so people are expected to choose work which yields the highest financial rewards. And we judge our standard of living by the amount of money we spend, imagining that the more we consume, the happier we will be. Yet once we regard ourselves as stewards, not owners, of our time and wealth, such a yardstick appears grossly inadequate. Certainly we each need to earn enough money to satisfy the basic needs of ourselves and our families. But work that is highly lucrative may also be environmentally destructive and socially unjust; equally the goods we consume may be ecologically harmful – and price is not always a good indication of quality.

Philip Neri, who founded a community in the sixteenth century whose members were scattered throughout Florence, required that his members turn the financial yardstick upside down: they should work as little as possible for money, and as much as possible for direct benefit – either of themselves or of their neighbours. His reasons were two-fold. Firstly the value of direct work can be clearly assessed since you can see its consequences, whereas work done for money draws you into the web of the national and international economy whose workings are quite impenetrable. Secondly direct mutual service within a family or neighbourhood draws people closer together in love and friendship, whereas when a person works for money he may never see the beneficiary of his labours.

Philip Neri's approach is far more radical and even revolutionary today than it was four hundred years ago. Now almost all our work is done for money, and many of us travel huge distances to the office or factory. Thus we buy almost everything we consume: even cooking is a dying art, as we rely increasingly on processed foods; and to relax we spend large sums on amusement parks, restaurants, hotels and all the other components of the modern leisure industry. As a consequence we are caught in the kind of moral trap which Philip Neri foresaw. By participating wholeheartedly in the money economy, we share responsibility for all the environmental destruction and material injustice which arises from the unconstrained pursuit of financial profit. Yet as individuals we are almost helpless in the face of such evil.

The modern application of Philip Neri's rule is to confine both work and consumption as far as possible to those spheres where the consequences can be perceived – and then to ensure that those consequences are good. Within the family this implies working for direct consumption: growing food in the garden; cooking from raw ingredients; maintaining the home; walking and cycling wherever possible, which takes more time but costs less money than driving; creating our own entertainment. Many of us can reduce our financial expenditure by a third or even a half by such means: not only are there direct savings, but we travel less, cutting into our largest single item of expenditure.

Beyond this we should, wherever the opportunity arises, prefer locally-produced goods to those imported from a far distance. And, where possible, we should make ourselves aware of how those goods are produced, buying only from firms who are themselves good stewards. By this means we as consumers can exert direct pressure on firms, eager for our custom, to be concerned for the environment.

Philip Neri required his members to devote one tenth of their time to charity, through giving either direct work or money

which they had earned. A married couple can follow the same
rule, but space their charitable activities over their whole lives.
With children at home many couples have little or no spare time
or money to give away. But they can make up for this in later
years when the children have left home, giving more liberally
than a single person because they can live more cheaply. Philip
Neri also recognized that all of us must at times be recipients
of the generosity of others, when we are old or sick. Rather
than resent such charity as a blow to our pride, we should offer
loving gratitude in return – which is the greatest of all gifts.

The good monk who is poor in spirit need not be materially
poor; and we who follow the monastic example of poverty
can enjoy true prosperity. A meal prepared from raw, organic
ingredients, especially if they are taken fresh from the garden,
is far tastier and more satisfying than the most costly processed
food from the supermarket. Leisure pursuits which draw families
and neighbours together, in each other's homes or in a local
field or hall, are far more enjoyable than the frenetic amusements
for which we must chase long distances and pay large sums.
And a home on which a couple has lavished both effort and
imagination is far more beautiful in their eyes than the luxuries
fashioned by others. Small wonder that monks have always been
envied for their good food, jovial recreation, and fine buildings.
The good steward in the world can share such riches.

## TASK

Write out a budget for a typical week, listing the items purchased and their cost. Then see how you could reduce expenditure, either by consuming less or by producing a substitute at home.

# FOOD

Eat food which the world regards as poor and dull, and you
will learn to enjoy food as much as a hungry family enjoys its
food.

Brigit

# FOOD

A few generations ago visitors to monasteries baulked at the austere food: heavy wholemeal bread; unpeeled potatoes; stews made from lentils and beans; and raw fruit at the end of each meal. For two thousand years anyone who could afford such luxuries ate white bread, peeled off the rough skin of root vegetables and the dark outer leaves of brassicas, avoided pulses and ate large amounts of meat instead, and preferred a cooked, sweet pudding to raw fruit. And by the early years of this century a combination of higher wages and mechanized food processing brought such a diet within the reach of ordinary people. Only the stricter monastic communities stuck firmly to the old peasant foods – on moral and spiritual grounds, rather than for reasons of nutrition, about which people remained largely ignorant.

Now, however, we know that the monastic diet is not only healthier, but also, once the palate has adjusted, tastier and more satisfying. We have realized that in refining our foods we destroy many of the vital elements which our bodies require, making us prone to a range of debilitating diseases. Moreover our preference for refined and sweetened foods arises from an unwitting self-deception, which ultimately reduces our enjoyment of food and tempts us towards obesity. The tongue naturally enjoys sweet foods because in the forest, where our sense of taste evolved, sweet roots and berries tend to be nutritious, while bitter or sour berries are usually poisonous – so the tongue guided our ancestors to eat good food. Sugar and white flour appeal to our desire for sweetness, but contain little or no nutrients – except for a high concentration of calories. We thus find ourselves eating far more calories than we need, causing us to grow fat; and, by overstimulating the palate, they reduce our enjoyment of the more subtle sweetness of fruit. The monastic diet, by contrast, is rich in the various vitamins, minerals and proteins which scientists have isolated. And its rough, bulky character makes the sin of gluttony far less tempting.

Nutrition, despite its great advances over the century, is a young science in which new discoveries are being made every decade; so our ignorance probably still far exceeds our knowledge. It is thus dangerous to base our diet purely on existing scientific knowledge, as many popular nutritionists advise. Rather we should try to eat naturally, consuming the food to which our primitive ancestors adapted, and which long monastic experience has proved to be nutritious. Natural food falls into three main categories. The first comprises fruit and vegetables. Our earliest forebears subsisted mainly on the berries they could pick from trees, and the tender roots they could pull up from the ground; and the earliest agriculture consisted simply in transferring young trees and vegetables to the land around a village, thus making it easier to collect food. The second category is seeds, both grains such as wheat and barley, and legumes such as beans and lentils. Picking seeds from wild grasses and bushes is a slow and laborious business, and the greatest advance in agriculture came when people began to clear ground and sow seed, harvesting their crop a few months later; by persistently retaining the biggest and juiciest seeds for sowing in the following year, our present range of grains and legumes were developed. The third category is meat. Our ancestors were skilled hunters, and then began to tame and rear their own animals; yet while meat – and fish near the coasts – was an important element in the primitive diet, it was rarely plentiful since hunting and animal husbandry are time-consuming occupations. We might add to this list milk, which has been taken from domestic animals for tens of thousands of years; eggs, which were lifted from nests before the era of domestic poultry; and honey, which was a much-prized delicacy.

Modern nutritional science assures us that such a diet contains all the nutrients which are currently known; more importantly, we can be sure that it also contains nutrients which have not yet been discovered, since the human body evolved to thrive on this natural range of foods. Our challenge is to re-educate our palates, so that we enjoy and relish the primitive diet. Aelred in the twelfth century wrote a moving description of the trauma he suffered moving from the king's palace in Scotland, where he held high office, to the monastery at Rievaulx: the hard bed, the rough clothes and the manual labour he could endure; but the dark bread, the thick lentil soup and the tough cabbage leaves made death by starvation seem attractive. Yet as Aelred and every other monk has found, after a few months the palate and the stomach adjust, so that natural foods actually give greater pleasure.

If we are to change our diet radically and to re-educate the palate, we must recognize how powerful is our attachment to refined, unnatural food. So the switch from one diet to another is likely to be as tough for us as it was for Aelred. The only successful way of making the change is to emulate Aelred by eliminating all temptations: in his case this meant living in a monastery, where he had no choice but to eat natural foods; in our case it means clearing all unnatural foods from the larder, apart perhaps from a few luxuries, and re-stocking it with natural foods. Happily a shopping list of raw vegetables and fruit, legumes and grains, with some meat and milk, proves far cheaper than the range of processed foods which most of us buy. So the bank balance will reveal an immediate reward for our efforts. And, since natural foods are far more bulky in relation to the calories they contain, we will find ourselves losing weight while still feeling full and satisfied with our meals – so those of us who are obese will receive further encouragement. But the greatest reward comes gradually as the weeks pass: the body feels healthier and meals become more enjoyable.

Monks have always fasted. In extreme cases this has meant forgoing food for days at a time; but more usually it implies giving up meat during Advent and Lent, as well as every Friday, and eating more sparingly of the other foods. The primary purpose is spiritual, to turn the focus of the mind inwards by taking away a major source of outward pleasure. There are, however, physical benefits too: the body actually gains vigour and energy, probably because it is free of the minor toxins that many foods, especially animal products, contain. In recent years many people have been rediscovering this old practice, finding that it is far less difficult than they had imagined. The occasional day without food at all suits some people – although, if you try this technique, it is vital to drink enough liquids. Becoming vegetarian during Advent and Lent is healthy, spiritually and physically, for us all.

If there are still large areas of ignorance about nutrition then the science of toxicology presents even greater mysteries. In particular we have little idea of the harm being inflicted on us by the innumerable chemicals now used in the cultivation and processing of food. Tests in laboratories may assure us that these chemicals are safe, but in practice it is virtually impossible to spot a long-term connection between particular chemicals and particular diseases. After all, it took four centuries of smoking to link tobacco with lung cancer, even though smoking is widespread and the correlation is strong; so there is little hope of proving a similar case against even a handful of food chemicals. Yet it is reasonable to imagine such connections exist. So our preference should always be for food which has been produced organically, with no chemical additives. Besides, organic cultivation benefits the soil, on which all life ultimately depends, while agricultural chemicals destroy it.

The great Irish abbess Brigit insisted that her nuns curbed their appetites in order to have ample food to give to the poor who came to their gates. Today the gross inequalities in food distribution are not local, but global, with entire nations and even continents suffering malnutrition, while others enjoy a surfeit. And since the global economy is so complex, there is no direct connection between us eating less and the starving of Africa having more. Nonetheless, natural foods, especially if only limited quantities of meat are eaten, make a much smaller claim on the earth's resources than artificial foods. And the money we save on the weekly shopping bill can, in part at least, be given for famine relief – as Brigit, if she were alive today, would surely urge.

## TASK

Clear out all unnatural foods from the larder, the fridge and the freezer – apart from two or three luxuries. Then restock with natural foods. Work out how much money is likely to be saved on the weekly food bill, which can then either be given to charity, or used as an opportunity to earn less from your paid work.

# GARDENING

The place in the monastery which is closest to God is not the church, but the garden. There the monks are at their happiest.

Pachomius

# GARDENING

To the Cornish monk Piran a well-kept garden was the perfect image of God's kingdom on earth: the plants and the soil which God has created are combined with the human imagination and skill which God inspires, to make a thing of heavenly beauty. Piran himself travelled the length and breadth of Cornwall, founding monasteries in which he and his followers laid out elaborate gardens of herbs, vegetables and flowers; and, so Piran believed, it was the admiration which these gardens evoked in Cornish hearts that converted many of them to Christianity.

Piran was a pioneer in a monastic tradition which has continued through sixteen centuries to the present day. Benedict prescribed gardening as part of the monks' daily routine; and by the seventh and eighth centuries Benedictine monasteries across Europe were exchanging herb and vegetable seeds, thereby introducing new varieties into their neighbourhoods. In the medieval period the Benedictines were famous for their wonderful herb gardens, laid out in elaborate patterns and often surrounded by a high wall – so on a hot afternoon the concentrated fragrance of the herbs could be quite overpowering. The herbs were used partly for cooking, but mainly for medicinal purposes, so that many monasteries functioned as herbal pharmacists, dispensing remedies to local people. Benedict's main emphasis, however, was on the work itself in cultivating vegetables and herbs: he believed that simple manual tasks were essential to the monk's physical and spiritual well-being. And, as Benedictine monks find to this day, wielding a hoe and a fork on a vegetable plot is the ideal activity for maintaining a strong back and supple limbs.

The monks in the early centuries used natural, organic methods of cultivation as a matter of course, because there was no choice: like all farmers then, they fertilized the soil with manure from their livestock and their own latrines, and they eliminated the weeds by hand. Today, while most farmers have replaced manual labour by chemicals and heavy machinery, most monasteries have retained their organic methods. They continue to make huge piles of manure outside the cow byre, and they continue to keep large compost bins to collect all natural refuse. Their one concession to modernity is perhaps a small tractor and trailer, so that in the autumn they can take the manure and compost to the garden without breaking their backs. Thus the monastery garden is not only beautiful, but is also an image of holiness, since in its cultivation it conforms to the laws of Nature – which are instituted by God.

To a visitor the typical monastery garden may seem large, but compared with the number of monks it is usually quite small. The reason is that, if the soil's fertility is maintained and the vegetables are planted thoughtfully, only a few square metres is needed to supply each person. Thus it is possible for almost all of us, even on quite modest means, to feed ourselves with wholesome organic vegetables, and to flavour our cooking with fresh herbs – and even to use our own herbal remedies for many common ailments. Those who are fortunate have their own gardens, so, like a monk in a monastery, they need only walk out of their back door to weed the row of carrots or dig potatoes. But in many towns and cities it is possible to rent small plots of land where vegetables can be grown, or take over a garden where owners regard it as a burden. And anyone can attach plant boxes to the outside of their windows in which a wide range of herbs can be cultivated.

Through long centuries of experience many monasteries have strong views on the tools that should be used in gardening. There are broadly two methods of turning the soil: to dig, using a spade or fork, with the downward force coming from the foot; or to 'chop', using a mattock, with the force coming from the whole body as the mattock is swung onto the soil. Most gardeners today use a spade or fork, but monks usually prefer mattocks. Digging compresses the spine, so making back injury far more likely; while swinging a mattock stretches the spine and strengthens the back muscles, reducing the danger of back injury. As a result back problems are comparatively rare in monasteries.

Monks are usually required to do at least two hours of manual work each day, which is far more than is necessary to maintain the garden. So they create flower beds, plant orchards of apples and plums, and look after the woodland in the monastery grounds. Most of us in modern towns and cities, with demanding jobs, could afford less than half that time for manual labour; but even so this is likely to leave ample spare time after the vegetables and herbs have been tended. Thus we can play our part in caring for the local environment. Churchyard, cemeteries, canal banks, woodland, playgrounds and school yards are all areas which too often become messy and unsightly through lack of care. We can thus volunteer our services at the weekend or on summer evenings to restore their beauty. In a monastery there are few finer sights than a small army of monks, with their habits tucked under their belts and with mattocks and shovels over their shoulders, marching out into the fields. We too can form similar holy armies, offering to fight the accumulation of rubbish in our neighbourhood and to care for its trees, shrubs and flowers.

# TASK

Calculate how much time on average you spend outdoors each week doing manual work. If it is less than six hours – the equivalent of one hour per working day – assess whether there are other opportunities for manual work, and how you could find time to engage in them.

# COOKING

The pots and pans used in the kitchen should be treated with the same respect as the sacred vessels of the altar.

Benedict

# COOKING

In Brigit's kitchen, in the monastery she founded in Ireland in the fifth century, a fire was always burning. This symbolized the flame of the Holy Spirit which came down upon the apostles at Pentecost, and which should burn with equal radiance in the heart of every monastery. But it also served a practical purpose. Suspended above the fire was a large cauldron in which pulses, root vegetables and grains were gently cooking. The nuns and monks ate from the cauldron each evening; and it provided hot food at any time of the day or night for strangers who called at the monastery. Moreover the monks and nuns needed to spend only a minimal time preparing food, simply tipping some more pulses, grains, vegetables and water into the cauldron each morning, so that they had ample time to care for the sick and the needy.

The human body, like that of all other creatures, evolved to consume food in its raw state, so our digestive system is far tougher and more effective at extracting nutrients from raw foods than is commonly supposed. Thus in Brigit's monastery, in addition to the stew from the cauldron, abundant raw fruit and green vegetables, as well as raw meat at festivals, was served. Cooking inevitably destroys some of the nutrients, especially of fruit and green vegetables; so we should continue to eat fruit and tender brassicas such as lettuce raw, while only cooking other green vegetables for the minimum time necessary to make them tender. But the invention of cooking, probably about twenty thousand years ago, greatly extended the range of foods human beings could consume. In particular the whole range of pulses and grain could now be heated in water, enhancing their taste and enabling them to be digested.

Brigit's method of cooking was that adopted by peasant households throughout medieval Europe. In the typical cottage a pot was kept permanently over the fire, gently simmering. In addition a flat stone stood at the edge of the fire, on which dough, made from rye and wheat, was rolled out, to become a rough bread. Richer households also had either a spit above the fire or a metal box beside it for roasting meat. In modern terminology these three methods of cooking are by radiation, as distinct from conduction – and thus conserve the nutrients. Conduction is where food has direct contact with the heat source, such as boiling and frying in which hot water or oil touch the food; the result is that much of the goodness of the food dissolves into the water or oil. Radiation, by contrast, is where the heat reaches the food indirectly, such as baking, roasting and stewing; although the heat itself destroys some nutrients, most of the goodness is unaffected.

Today, of course, we no longer have open fires on which to cook. But it is quite possible in the modern kitchen to emulate Brigit. The ideal instrument is the flat-topped cooker which is kept permanently hot by solid fuel or oil. Bread can be baked in the hot oven, pulses and whole grains can be stewed slowly in the warm oven, meat can be roasted by transferring it at the optimum moment from the hot to the warm oven (so the internal temperature does not rise above 85°C), and vegetables can be steamed or baked. Unfortunately such cookers are expensive to buy, and, unless one is cooking for large numbers, expensive to run. The same results can be achieved more cheaply with an electric slow cook-pot for stewing the pulses and a microwave oven for the vegetables – with a conventional oven for baking and roasting.

For many people who wish to cook using natural, raw ingredients, the greatest problem is the time itself. The numerous recipes for healthy dishes mostly involve at the very least an hour or two in the kitchen – which people with demanding jobs or young children at their heels cannot afford to give. Thus, despite their preference to the contrary, they continue to use processed foods. The monastic cookery of Brigit, however, is extremely quick, taking no more time than using processed food; all that it requires is a degree of planning. Pulses and whole grains are

Nature's own convenience foods, since only water needs to be added, with some salt, herbs and oil to enhance the flavour – and six hours later a perfect stew is ready. As in the typical monastery larder, we should have a row of large jars containing a range of pulses and grains: lentils, yellow peas, kidney beans, marrowfat peas, whole wheat and barley, rice – there is a large choice. In the evening or early morning put two kinds of pulse and a whole grain into the pot; add one or two types of herb and enough salt and oil to draw out the taste; then pour in ample water and place it into the warm oven or slow cooker. It does not matter what time dinner is eaten, since the stew will be ready after four or five hours, and remain equally delicious for at least twenty-four hours. Experience soon teaches the optimum amount of water, oil and salt – but it is best to err on the generous side for all three, for such cooking is often ruined by making the stew too dry or bland. The best and quickest way of cooking vegetables is to chop them up, with the minimum amount of prior washing and peeling, and then put them in the microwave or hot oven with a small amount of water at the bottom of the dish.

The way we produce, prepare and serve food is fundamental to our relationship with the natural order, with one another, and with God. Bad farming practice is one of the greatest threats to the ecology of our planet, destroying fauna and flora of every kind and eroding the soil. Thus consuming food which we know has been grown organically is a small contribution to the saving of our planet; and if enough people do the same, farmers will be compelled to revive organic methods of cultivation. The increasingly prevalent habit of 'grazing', in which members of a family wander into the kitchen whenever they are hungry, to re-heat processed good, and then sit down in front of the television to eat it, is a threat to the integrity of the family. The family meal each evening, prepared with love and eaten together, has for twenty thousand years been the central act of the day, enabling parents and children, brother and sister, husband and wife, to celebrate their unity, and to share events and experience. Our affluence, in which we have come to take the gift of food for granted, is a spiritual threat, tempting us to ignore God's providence; and the decline of the habit of offering a prayer of blessing before meals is a sign that we are succumbing to the temptation. Benedict believed that every meal should be regarded as an act of worship in which we give thanks to God for food and thence for all his blessings, and ask that we may be strengthened for his service. If we at home consume good wholesome food, in an atmosphere of love, and if we can restore the habit of prayer before eating, even if it is only a few moments of silence, then each meal shall become, in Benedict's phrase, a 'holy communion' – a communion of Nature, Mankind and God.

## TASK

Compose or find a grace which you can say before a meal – or find a traditional grace with which you feel comfortable. And then use that grace at least once a week, preferably when you are eating with family or friends. One possible grace is that composed by St Patrick of Ireland: 'Bless this food for our use, and us for your service. Amen.'

# HOME

The beauty of our shared home should reflect the beauty of the love contained within its walls.

Teresa

# HOME

The monks sought simplicity and poverty, and yet constructed some of the finest and most beautiful buildings of the entire world. Most of the cathedrals of Europe are – or were – monastic foundations; and where the cloisters, dormitories, refectories and other monastic buildings survive, clustered round a great cathedral, we can glimpse the most nearly perfect environment which the human species has ever created. If we cast our gaze more widely to include other religious traditions, there too the monastic architects displayed sublime genius: the Buddhist monasteries of south-east Asia, and the Sufi mosques of the Middle East, are as breathtaking as Chartres or Fountains.

The solution to this paradox – of austere poverty combined with sumptuous beauty – can be found in the architecture itself. The most splendid and awe-inspiring monastery is also homely and restful, as if God and man are beautifully brought together in the stones and mortar. And as one studies more closely the shape and form of the monastic buildings, one can see how harmoniously they fit into their natural surroundings, following the contour of the land or nestling into rugged hillsides, and using for the most part local materials – as if God himself had built them at the creation. Thus the monks in the glorious buildings remain poor in spirit, in the sense that those buildings do not defy Nature, but rather enhance her beauty, and thus bring their inhabitants into closer harmony with her.

Moreover in a crude economic sense good buildings are cheap. The cost of any good building is based not merely on the resources used in its production, but also on its durability: the longer a good building will last, the cheaper it becomes, since its cost of production can be spread more thinly. By this calculation our ancient monastic buildings, which in their construc-

tion required whole armies of masons and carpenters, have
proved a remarkably light economic burden.

We today should display the same love of architectural beauty,
and make the same calculation. It is tempting to suppose that
the monk in the world, committed to poverty and simplicity,
should have shabby, meagre accommodation, with shoddy furniture and drab decoration. Yet the shabbiest buildings, with damp
flimsy walls, are ludicrously expensive to heat; and since they
survive only a few short decades, they are exceedingly wasteful
of both materials and labour. Worse still, ugliness corrodes the
human spirit, destroying its natural vitality and joy. Thus poor
buildings do not encourage holy poverty. Instead we should
willingly lavish effort and money on fine, solid homes, containing strong, well-proportioned furniture – knowing that by this
means we are conserving, not wasting, the earth's resources.

In practice, of course, most of us must buy or rent houses
built by others, so we have no direct control over their building.
But we can determine the type of house we buy; and ultimately,
if enough of us make the right choices, builders will be compelled
to take notice. Today the single most important criterion in our
decision should be energy efficiency, since the profligate use of
energy is the greatest ecological threat to our planet. Thus we
should check both that the house is well-insulated, and that its
main rooms face south, enabling the warmth of the sun to save
fuel costs. Then we should require durable construction so that,
even if the house will not match a cathedral's longevity, it will
welcome five or ten generations across its threshold.

And we should also, like the monk, choose a home that is
pleasing to the eye, and hence to the heart. In recent decades,
dazzled by its own technological abilities, the Western world
has thrown aside traditional architectural styles, and created
quite new types of homes – of which the apartment in a multi-
story block is the most extreme. The mistake, which has led to
so much misery, has been to imagine our generation knows
more about beauty and comfort than its ancestors. In fact good
architecture has always been traditional, even nostalgic, constantly adopting and adapting old styles. Even those magnificent
cathedrals and abbeys of the medieval period deliberately used

classical methods and forms of construction; and Victorian architecture, which we are at last learning to appreciate, consciously
adopted medieval styles. The monk in the world need feel no
shame in living in a quaint old cottage, or a modern house built
to traditional standards.

Monastic rules and guides have always emphasized the importance of keeping the monastery neat and tidy; and visitors to
monasteries through the centuries have always been impressed
at how clean they were kept. Yet monks and nuns have never
spent much time doing housework, and no rule mentions cleaning as an important part of the daily routine. The reason is that
monasteries are furnished very simply, even austerely, so that
rooms can be cleaned quickly. Most modern homes, by contrast,
are cluttered with furniture much of which serves little purpose;
every shelf and mantelpiece is filled with ornaments; and there
are numerous cupboards stuffed with utensils, appliances and
miscellaneous objects collected over the years, the bulk of which
are never used. As a consequence housework is exceedingly
complex and laborious, requiring many hours each week.

The answer is to go through the house every year, inspecting
each article of furniture, each utensil, each article of clothing –
each object in every room – and ask whether it has been used
during the past twelve months. If not, it should either be given
away or thrown away. At first discarding old belongings, even
if they have neither use nor sentimental attachment, will involve
a mental struggle, because the acquisitive and possessive spirit is
exceedingly strong in modern culture. But once the home is
cleared of surplus goods, there will be a sense of freedom, as if
a heavy burden has been unloaded. And the time spent doing
housework is cut to only a couple of hours at most each week.
A mantelpiece, which when filled with ornaments took five
minutes to clean, now takes five seconds; and a floor, which
was a jungle of furniture legs taking twenty minutes to vacuum,
now requires two or three. What is more, a room containing
only a few items of furniture and ornament, each of the finest
quality, is a far more restful place in which to sit than the junk-
shops which most of us inhabit.

## TASK

Look at all the shelves in your home, and inside all your cupboards, and take away everything which is neither useful nor has any real sentimental value. If a utensil or gadget has not been used in the past year, throw it out. Observe how much easier and quicker it is to keep your home clean. Give to charity all the things you discard.

# WORK

Every monk must share in the daily toil, working with his hands. Since idleness is the mother of petty gossip and quarrels, so all must labour so hard that they want only to love one another. They should dig the ground with mattocks and shovels, wield hoes to cut weeds and axes to chop wood, and provide for themselves all the necessities of life.

David

# WORK

In the traditional Benedictine monastery the monk changes his occupation at least every one and a half hours. This prevents him ever becoming bored by a single monotonous activity. And it ensures that in the course of each day a variety of gifts and abilities, both physical and mental, are exercised. Thus in a typical morning he may sing lustily in the chapel choir, dig vigorously in the vegetable garden, read a profound work of philosophy, and welcome a group of visitors. And after a hearty lunch and a nap, he may give a lecture to a group of novices, help cook the evening meal, bring the cows in for milking, and sing yet more glorious hymns and psalms in chapel. Small wonder that monks have always been renowned for their    .ldy faces, glowing health and startling longevity.

The monks' diversity of activities is natural to the human species. Our primitive ancestors in the forest had to hunt wild animals, gather wild fruits and vegetables, repair their mud and grass huts, fashion tools and weapons, and chop trees for firewood. And, although all these tasks were phsyically arduous, they also required great intelligence and dexterity. Yet, far from absorbing all their time and energy, they found ample time to play with their children, to tell stories to one another, to dance and sing at festivals, and even to paint their own bodies and the walls of caves. They too can rarely have spent more than ninety minutes on a single occupation; and each day all their gifts and abilities were fully stretched.

Today most of us are required to do a single task for seven or eight hours each day, and for five days each week. Indeed, so dominant is that job in our lives that we tend to identify ourselves by it when we introduce ourselves to others. And the majority of jobs in the modern economy are sedentary, using almost exclusively the logical faculty of the mind, while leaving the body to atrophy, and the intuition and imagination to languish.

In our younger years we can usually accept our lot quite happily. The body retains much of the strength and suppleness of childhood, despite lack of use. And the financial rewards, combined with hopes of promotion, seem adequate compensation for the monotony of much of our work. Moreover, we still have ample energy to enjoy ourselves in the evenings and at weekends. But as the years pass, we find ourselves increasingly frustrated and dissatisfied. Despite working far shorter hours than our primitive ancestors, we often feel utterly exhausted at the end of the day and of the week, because that part of ourselves which the job uses has been stretched beyond its natural limit. And at the same time we find ourselves yearning for fresh activities and fresh challenges, knowing that our exhaustion would disappear, like a burden dropping from our backs, if other faculties and abilities were brought into use. The mid-life crisis, which so many of us experience, is the moment when our eyes focus on the gilded cage we have constructed around ourselves – and like an animal in a zoo, we roar with angry despair.

At first the bars of the cage may seem impossibly thick and strong, precluding all hope of escape. And, besides, we may feel so dependent on the comforts and safety of the cage itself that we dare not risk any change. Yet to be a monk in the world does not require us to force our way out, nor to abandon every comfort. The cage is largely within the mind: it consists of our belief, engendered by the society in which we live, that work implies a single paid profession with which we identify. Once we allow ourselves to question that belief, the cage widens and extends, until it becomes a light fence around a large field, offering ample space to exercise all our abilities.

We must begin simply by reducing the number of hours spent at our main job. At first this may seem a frightening prospect, both because our salary will fall, and because prospects of promotion may be marred. But the real cut in income is less than the crude figure suggests: we may find ourselves travelling less, especially if we can actually reduce the number of days at work and so save on petrol and fares; and, if we are more relaxed and fulfilled, we want to spend less money on luxuries – which we buy mainly to assuage our discontent. As for promotion, employers often find that part-time workers are more productive and efficient than full-time staff, because they have more energy and enthusiasm. So the more of us that take the step of reducing our working hours, the more firms will recognize the value of encouraging and promoting part-time staff.

Once the step is taken, not only are there more hours in the day for other activities, but also the burden of continuous exhaustion falls away, leaving us free to develop new arts and new skills. Like the monk, each day should contain both manual and mental work. So if the paid job is mental, then it is important to find a garden or allotment to cultivate; and in every neighbourhood there are elderly, disabled or sick people whose own gardens need tending and whose houses need decorating. And we should follow the monastic example in setting aside ample time for meditation and study, reading books that not only interest and entertain us, but also deepen our understanding of the mysteries of God's creation. Perhaps too there is opportunity for imaginative expression: if even the most unmusical monk in the medieval monastery could learn plainchant, then all of us can find some artistic endeavour that unlocks the imagination.

Our primitive ancestors lived within close-knit communities, whose customs and traditions defined each person's activities from dawn until dusk. The monastery recreates such a community, with bells chiming to tell the monks when to move from one occupation to another. But the monk in the world has neither community nor bells to order his time. And when we reduce the number of hours in paid employment, we are liable simply to fritter away the extra time. So we must set ourselves a timetable, at least from the early morning until the late afternoon – and stick to the timetable with religious devotion. In making the timetable, the monastic rule should apply, that ninety minutes, or at most two hours, should be given to each occupation. And as far as possible each day should contain both mental and manual activities – and also both social and solitary activities.

## TASK

Talk over with your spouse or a friend your stewardship of time and talents, asking whether the work you do is satisfying and healthy for yourself, and of value to others. If on reflection you feel you are misusing your time and talents to some degree, try to plan what realistic changes you can make.

# SECURITY

The poor monk is lord of the world. He has handed over all his cares to God, and so can enjoy all the beauty and the bounty of God's creation.

Francis

# SECURITY

When St Anthony walked out into the desert, he had no idea of where he could find food and drink. And the Celtic monks, like St Brendan, who set sail from the shores of Britain and Ireland in tiny coracles, did not know whether they would reach land before their meagre supplies ran out. To these early monastic heroes such foolhardy adventures were acts of faith, in which they threw themselves totally on the mercy of God.

We today, by contrast, enjoy as much material security and safety as this world can afford. We have no anxieties about food since the shops around us are all amply stocked. And if our own harvest fails, our government has ample surplus stocks, and also ample money to purchase additional food from outside. Water is available at the turn of a tap, and light and heat fill our homes at the flick of a switch. We live in houses so solidly built that they can withstand the most violent hurricanes. Moreover, if disaster should strike, we are insured: a bad injury which interrupts our work, a fire in the home, or a road accident which damages the car, can all be provided for by making modest payments to an insurance company.

At first sight such security seems to contradict any desire for poverty and simplicity. Besides, Nature herself is uncertain and unstable, so that our tribal and peasant ancestors suffered perpetual anxiety that their crops would be destroyed by drought, disease or storm – and they would be faced with famine. So the risks of Anthony and Brendan did not seem so extreme to their contemporaries as they do to us. If, therefore, we are to live as monks in the world, it may seem that any kind of insurance or provision for the future should be rejected – including, even, saving for a retirement pension.

The monastic way is not, however, as reckless as the examples of Anthony and Brendan suggest. Once monks began to form communities under Pachomius, and later under Benedict, they could support one another through difficulties and disaster. If a monk fell sick or was injured, he was looked after by his brethren. If his cell collapsed during a high wind, his brethren shared in rebuilding it. And the monastery as a whole owned sufficient land that they could plant a wide variety of crops; so if one or two failed, they could be sure that others would bear a harvest. Not surprisingly medieval peasants often envied the material security of the monastery – and undoubtedly one of the reasons why so many people in medieval times were prepared to endure the rigours of monastic life was to share this security.

At a purely economic level the insurance company imitates the monastic community. By inviting a large group of people to contribute to a common fund, the insurance company can provide for any members of that group who suffer particular hardships. The insurance company is thus an invisible community which pools the risks of its subscribers. In a modern economy the government also supplies insurance, not only through welfare payments to the unemployed and elderly, but also through the provision of hospitals and schools. The cost of treating sickness and educating children can be so high that few individuals could afford it out of current income. Thus, by levying taxes on people throughout their lives, the government can give these services to people, without direct charge, when they need them. Indeed, so deeply embedded is the principle of insurance in our society, that none of us can avoid it.

The danger of insuring against disaster and providing for the future lies not in the actions themselves, but in the attitude that they can engender. With our abundant stocks of food, our unshakeable houses, our insurance against disaster, plus the welfare services of the state, we imagine ourselves to be in command of our destiny – or at least well protected from adversity. Comparing ourselves with our primitive ancestors, or with the impoverished masses of Africa and Asia, we take pride in our mastery over Nature. Yet, as anyone who has travelled amongst the poor of Africa and Asia will know, their hospitality and generosity puts us to shame: they readily share what little they have with the stranger or the friend in need, while our homes are fortresses against the demands of others. And the poor too possess a spontaneity which we have lost, responding to opportunities to help others or simply to enjoy themselves without thought of the cost. Our illusion that we can control our lives stifles these natural impulses.

Worse still, this illusion cuts us off from God. Our ancestors, acutely aware of the uncertainties of daily life, constantly turned to God in prayer. They asked God's blessing on their crops, and poured out their gratitude to him after the harvest. When a woman was giving birth they begged God for a safe delivery, and when anyone fell sick they invoked God's healing power. When they travelled, they stopped at every church they passed, opening the south door to say a prayer to St Christopher, the patron saint of travellers, whose picture was invariably painted on the north wall. And on rising, eating and preparing for sleep, they put themselves in God's hands. Such constant prayer was not a sign of peculiar holiness, but of the palpable truth that only divine power could protect them against danger – God was their insurance policy. Few of us now place such trust in God, because we have faith in our ability to protect ourselves.

In recent years, however, the illusion of control has begun to crack. While as individuals we can insure ourselves against catastrophe, as a species we remain highly vulnerable. Indeed in our efforts to become master of Nature, we are destroying her bounty on which our lives depend. Through pollution, through the destruction of fauna and flora, and through the depletion of mineral resources, we are in danger of bringing upon ourselves and our dependants permanent famine and pestilence. As yet western living standards have remained untouched by the gathering ecological crisis. But there is now little doubt that, if our economic activities continue unchecked, the crisis will break over the heads of our children and grandchildren.

Monastic literature is filled with exhortations to monks and nuns that they should love and cherish God's creation, caring for the animals and birds in their charge as God's own children, and seeking constantly to maintain and enhance the fertility of the soil they cultivate. Indeed, throughout the medieval period the monasteries were pioneers in agriculture, developing new systems of ploughing and irrigation. To the monks such an attitude towards the natural order was a matter of faithful obedience, since God himself had instituted the laws of Nature. And they believed that if they disobeyed those laws, Nature herself would rise up and punish them by destroying their crops.

If we today are to learn afresh how to live in harmony with Nature, we must begin by acknowledging the limits of our powers – and thus to realize that, left to ourselves, our material wellbeing is extremely insecure. Then our hearts will rediscover the generosity and spontaneity of our primitive ancestors – and of the monks of old.

## TASK

Spend a few minutes in silence, imagining yourself in the position of a peasant farmer in medieval Europe, or in modern Africa or Asia, entirely dependent on the vagaries of the weather for your survival. Reflect on how this affects your attitude to Nature, and to life itself.

# CLOTHES

We can look as fine as the richest nobility if we wear with
humility and grace the simple garments of a lowly peasant.

Catherine

# CLOTHES

Many of the earliest monks who trekked out into the Egyptian and Syrian desert in the steps of St Anthony wore only loincloths, regarding nakedness as part of their vow of poverty. During the day the fierce sun burned their bare skin, while in the chilly desert night they shivered. St Benedict, however, in his communities in Italy, imposed a more gentle regime, in the hope that more ordinary people might be attracted to the monastic life. He stipulated that his monks should wear a simple habit, made from coarse woollen cloth. The habit should not be tailored to suit the individual monk's figure, but should hang loose like a sack, with a rope round the middle to prevent it flapping in the breeze. And it was not to be dyed, but should remain the colour which the sheep themselves provided. Thus the monks were warm at night, and protected from the sun by day; but there was no temptation to vanity.

The Benedictine habit has been the costume of monks ever since. For many centuries the monks in a monastery would display a variety of different colours, reflecting the various natural colours of sheep. But by the medieval period, as distinct religious orders were formed, each order specified particular colours. Some wore white, some brown or black, and others a mixture of colours. The rule against dyes remained, so these uniforms depended on each monastery keeping sheep of the right shade. Moreover each order developed its own way of cutting the cloth, giving the habit its special style. As a result the monastic habit acquired a simple beauty and elegance; and a group of monks, processing in their identical habits down the nave of their chapel, was a veritable feast to the eye.

Personal vanity, which the monks strived to suppress within themselves, is a natural human emotion. Just as many species of animal and bird preen themselves, especially as part of their courtship rituals, so human beings have always wanted to enhance the beauty of their bodies. Tribal peoples may paint their torsoes in bright colours, and wear elaborate headdresses of coloured feathers; while the modern Westerner pays large sums to have his or her hair cut and permed into strange shapes, and spends large amounts on clothes of every hue and style. The biological purpose of our vanity is to attract a mate, so that – as monastic writers have always recognized – our desire for fine clothes has a sexual connotation. Yet the vanity remains long after courtship has ceased, so that even an elderly widow, for whom thoughts of mating are quite remote, may devote infinite care to her wardrobe.

A married couple would be wrong to follow the monk in defying their natural vanity. If a marriage is to remain warm and vibrant, husband and wife must continue to make themselves attractive to each other. Indeed when a couple become careless about their appearance to one another, it is often a sign that their relationship is crumbling. Yet such benign vanity need not imply high expenditure nor anxiety to keep up with the latest fashions. Just as a monk can look beautiful in a woollen habit, if it is skilfully cut and is kept clean, so we too can look quite elegant and attractive in simple clothes. Garments that are both comfortable and shapely, and are dyed in shades that reflect the colours of nature, enhance the beauty of the human body.

Happily we are endowed with an instinct which guides our dress-sense. We feel awkward and embarrassed in clothes that are either dowdy or flamboyant. But we feel easy and confident in clothes that possess a natural elegance. If we constantly defy the instinct, by spending either too much or too little attention to our appearance, the instinct soon becomes distorted, and so fails to guide our choice of clothing. If, however, we submit to this instinct, we shall look as fine as a peacock – or a Benedictine monk.

The monk's habit, as well as being simple and elegant, serves a further important purpose: it signals to people he meets – and also to himself – his particular vocation. Thus if we meet in a train compartment a man in a brown habit with a rope girdle round his waist and sandals on his feet, we know that we can talk to him about spiritual and moral concerns – and receive a warm, sympathetic response. Equally the monk himself, wearing such garb in a public place, is sharply aware of his own identity, and thence the behaviour that is expected of him. In the privacy of the monastery, with only other monks for company, he can forget himself. But in any other context his habit is a powerful symbol.

The clothes which the rest of us wear may be less conspicuous in a train compartment, but are no less symbolic. Dressing with simple, natural elegance conveys a message to others about our values – that we seek to be simple and natural in life as a whole. Equally dowdiness or flamboyance carry a negative message. The symbolic function of clothes does, however, confront us with a sartorial problem which the monk escapes. The monk's work is encompassed within the life of the monastery, so the same style of clothes is suitable at all times. But many of us with jobs in the world are expected to adopt forms of dress at work, which may seem to conflict with our desire for simplicity. A male doctor or solicitor, to inspire confidence in the patient or client, must wear an expensive dark suit; while his female colleague must spend even more on a range of costly outfits, never wearing the same garments for more than two or three days in a row. Rather than cause needless offence by rejecting these conventions, it is wisest to regard such clothes as the monk regards costly vestments to be worn when celebrating Holy Communion – as desirable extravagances in the service of God and humanity.

The monastic habits were, of course, always spun and woven by the monks themselves, using wool from their own sheep. Few of us today can keep sheep in our gardens, but the crafts of spinning and weaving, as well as knitting, are happy occupations during dark winter evenings. Moreover, as a concession to marital vanity, we can dye our yarn in a range of delicate hues, using all sorts of natural substances, from onion peelings to moss scraped from rocks. A jersey or a shawl which has been spun, knitted and dyed by hand far surpasses the most costly product of a fashionhouse in beauty and elegance – and sexiness.

## TASK

Look through your wardrobe. Ask which clothes feel natural and right, being both elegant and simple – as well as comfortable. Then give away the rest. You may be surprised how many clothes you give away, but you will not miss them.

# MEDIA

Since the world was created by God, it is an act of worship to describe the world in paint or in words.

Pachomius

# MEDIA

A visitor in medieval times, walking round the cloister of a great abbey, would have found a dozen or more monks perched on high stools, leaning over a piece of parchment on a desk. Some would have been copying the Scriptures, or a devotional book, in the most perfect italic hand. Others would have been painting exquisite pictures to illustrate these books, or to paste on to wooden boards in parish churches. If the visitor had proceeded to the monastery workshops, he would have found other monks painting much larger pictures to be included in chancel screens, carving statues of Jesus, Mary and the saints, or even fashioning musical instruments to be played during services. Later, during the recreation period after the evening meal, the visitors might have heard monks telling each other stories, some hilariously funny and others thrilling or tragic.

Artistic expression – painting pictures, carving sculptures, making music, writing books, telling stories – are natural human activities. In the most primitive tribal societies people paint portraits of animals and trees on cave walls and pieces of bark, they turn tree trunks into divine images, and they make simple harps and violins from wooden sticks and pieces of leather. And in the evenings the old men hold the children spellbound by mythical stories of former glories and tragedies, handed down through countless generations. Every human being has a vivid imagination, which needs to be fed – and which needs to feed others.

Printing was, of course, the first mass medium of communication, enabling books to be produced so cheaply and quickly that even quite humble families could afford them. Monasteries were quick to grasp the power of this new technology, as a means of disseminating Christian ideas; and so in the larger communities a printing-press was soon installed, and monks were trained to operate this. But printing made the monastic scribes redundant; and thus, by undermining one of the essential social functions of the monastery, it may have contributed to the decline of monasticism in the sixteenth century.

The modern electronic media, radio and television, magnify a hundredfold the challenges and dangers of printing. Today a small group of professionals in a television studio can provide pictures, music and stories of the highest artistic quality, to be broadcast to millions of homes. Thus the artistic endeavours of ordinary people seem feeble and even valueless by comparison. Moreover the continuous output of radio and television can tempt us to spend hour upon hour each day as passive recipients of the artistic talents of others, while leaving our own talents to lie idle. This corrosive power of the electronic media has been augmented by modern factory technology, which can reproduce pictures and sculptures almost perfectly, as well as provide wall-papers, carpets and furnishing fabrics of every description with which to adorn our home. So, faced with such superior quality at quite low prices, there is little incentive for the amateur craftsman.

Just as the late medieval monasteries appreciated the power of printing, many modern monasteries have reflected deeply on how to handle the modern media. A few have barred radio and television altogether. The majority, however, have found ways of being both discriminating and restrained in their use of radio and television, so that their impact is almost wholly benign. Within the tight monastic routine television can only be watched in the hours of recreation in the early evening, which limits potential viewing. But as many an abbot and abbess has recognized, the types of programmes at that time are often far from uplifting. The video recorder has solved the problem in many cases, enabling good documentaries and dramas to be taped, and then re-played during the recreation period. Another piece of modern technology which has brought spiritual benefits is the small radio with earphones. A remarkable number of monasteries allow their members to listen to the news bulletins at night, to give them subjects for prayer. Many monks take notes during the bulletins, to ensure they remember all the national and international problems correctly – with the result that monks are often remarkably well-informed!

The average West European and American now spends around three and a half hours per day watching television, plus a further two hours listening to the radio. Undoubtedly television has broadened our intellectual horizons, so that even small children are remarkably knowledgeable about the plight of the African elephant or the depletion of the ozone layer. Yet the sheer quantity of time which the electronic media absorb precludes many of the creative activities which our ancestors enjoyed – from inventing games and telling stories, to making music and writing letters, let alone painting and carving. The monasteries enable these individual artistic endeavours to continue unimpeded because television and radio are confined to hours which would otherwise be spent chatting or even dozing. The monk in the world has no alternative but to exercise a similar discipline over his viewing and listening, in order to give full expression to the artistic talents which God has bestowed.

The modern monastery has also tamed another modern form of communication, which is even more intrusive than the television. In the modern home and office the telephone has undermined the most basic tenet of good manners, interrupting with its insistent ring the most intimate and important conversation. Moreover it can destroy the quiet rhythm of work, prayer and recreation, reducing our efficiency and our equanimity. Many monasteries resisted for decades having a telephone installed, requiring that all communication with the outside world be confined to letters. When they finally gave way they ensured that the telephone could be disconnected during time of prayer and meals, only answering it at specified hours of the day. Now the automatic answering machine can achieve the same result.

It takes a surprising degree of self-control not to answer the telephone: as a culture we have come to take for granted its bad manners. Yet if, like monks, we designate only an hour or two each day when we respond to its call, then we have broken the tyranny. Relatives, friends and colleagues soon get to know the periods when they can expect an answer, and time their calls accordingly. In the meantime an answering machine can take the strain. For vital calls from one's spouse or children a simple signal can be agreed to ensure one answers – such as allowing the telephone to ring once, then ringing off and dialling again immediately. The telephone then becomes a welcome friend, rather than a rude intruder.

## TASK

Remove the television for a week. See which programmes you really miss, and which you can happily forget. Then when you restore the television, only watch the programmes you missed. Also unplug the telephone, except for specified hours – which you can let your friends and relatives know. You may find that this arrangement proves such a blessing that you want to adopt it permanently.

# HEALTH

We should not show an excessive preoccupation with the needs of the body. But we should do all that is necessary to preserve the body's health and strength, in order to serve God to the best of our abilities.

Ignatius

# HEALTH

Monks were renowned for their longevity. While the ordinary people of the towns and villages of medieval Europe could expect to die by the age of forty, monks typically lived out their full span of three score years and ten – or even longer. They were more resistant to the plague and the myriad other diseases which carried people to an early grave; and even if they were infected, they were more likely to survive. At the time the cause of their rude health was assumed to be celibacy: by refraining from sexual activity, they were assumed to be retaining the natural forces of life. But now in retrospect it is clear that the secret lay in the food they ate, the work they did, and the routine they followed.

Today we can all expect to live our full span, like the monks of old. But we cannot necessarily expect to remain healthy throughout life. In many areas and workplaces a tenth or even a fifth of people fail to appear for work on a typical day, suffering from some minor malady. Viruses and infections of all kinds spread rapidly through neighbourhoods; chronic ailments such as back pain, asthma and migraine are perpetual sources of discomfort for countless thousands; and many people without any recognized condition pass much of their life feeling poorly. We are inclined to regard frequent or chronic illness as an inevitable part of normal life; and four, five or six visits to the doctor each year cause no surprise. Indeed in most Western countries as much as a tenth of the economy is devoted to medical care; and doctors have largely taken over from priests as the people to whom we turn in time of need – to provide pills and potions to relieve our distress.

The contrast with the rest of God's creation could hardly be more striking. Certainly animals and birds can contract diseases in the natural world. But this is the exception, not the rule;

and unless attacked by predators, the great majority of God's creatures live out their natural span in good health. And when we ourselves own animals as pets, we quite properly try to imitate their natural conditions in the food we give them and in their activities. Indeed we would regard it as cruel to feed a dog on a diet of chocolate and the other sweet things which he enjoys; and to deprive a dog of exercise is rightly condemned. On the contrary we know that a dog's health depends on it consuming a natural diet of meat, and having ample opportunity to run wild in the park. And under such conditions we can expect our pets to remain sleek and healthy almost to the day they die.

Oddly the aspect of monastic life to which people ascribed the monks' good health, celibacy, is its least natural feature. In other respects they created a pattern of existence which in its essence imitated Nature. The simple food they grew and ate was little different from that of our primitive ancestors in the forest. And their emphasis on frugality meant that they ate sparingly – as our ancestors were forced to do. They had plenty of exercise, tilling the soil and tending livestock, to keep their bodies fit and trim. And they enjoyed a steady routine, without unnecessary and undue stress.

The longevity which we experience today is not due to the healthiness of our way of life, but to the extraordinary progress in the past century in medical research, yielding a vast range of drugs to combat almost every illness. Yet paradoxically this progress contributes to our ill health. From the first weeks of life our bodies are bombarded with alien chemicals, which may cure a specific problem, but must inevitably undermine the body's natural resistance and strength. Doctors may reassure us, quite sincerely, that particular drugs have few or no immediate side effects; but they cannot measure or calculate the long-term damage to our general state of health of the numerous different potions we ingest. And the fact that historically monks and nuns have enjoyed far better health than we do, with only a few herbal remedies for their occasional ailments, suggests strongly that the specific benefits of drugs are largely outweighed by the general harm. Indeed, as many doctors now acknowledge, most common ailments are healed by the body itself – and so the wise patient should only consent to take medicine for the more serious illness. Thus our best hope of living the full span, and enjoying good health until the final weeks and days, is to trust Nature's way, resorting to drugs only in extreme circumstances.

While the bulk of monks have enjoyed healthy natural lives, there have always been some who imagine it to be holy to deprive their bodies, eating bad food, forgoing exercise, and subjecting themselves to extreme nervous stress, in pursuit of some divine mission. Equally there are innumerable people today who knowingly lead unhealthy lives, subsisting on 'fast', processed foods, and passing the entire day in an office chair or at the wheel of a car, relentlessly seeking profit and success. Psychologically both the immoderate monk and the over-ambitious businessman suffer the same disorder: at heart they dislike and despise themselves, and so refuse to care for their bodies – making mission or career the excuse for their self-hatred. It is a pattern of behaviour and an excuse to which all of us should be alert, since we can all at times be tempted towards self-hatred. And we should see it as a duty towards God, not an indulgence of the flesh, to care for our bodies: since he created us and loves us, we should love ourselves.

In recent decades, as growing numbers have realized that our unnatural way of life is responsible for many of our ailments, numerous schemes for diet and exercise have been promulgated. Some dietary evangelists advocate eating only raw food, some urge reductions in fat or salt, others see lack of roughage as the cause of our problems. Exercise evangelists similarly focus on particular activities or movements which, if practised a few times each day, will make the body lithe and supple. While most of these schemes undoubtedly contain elements of truth, they are often mutually contradictory, and based on scant research. Since the workings of the body are so complex and mysterious, it is unlikely that we shall devise a diet or a system of physical exercise that can be proven as perfect. Rather, we should admit our ignorance, and recognize that our best guide is history. The monks themselves wanted to retreat from the unhealthy sophistication of urban civilization, to the primitive simplicity of their ancestors. In the process they created a civilization of their own which was itself quite sophisticated – but which succeeded in emulating the diet and the activities of our forebears. Similarly we cannot return to some primitive, natural state; but we can, like the monks, ensure that our artificial way of life conforms as closely as possible to natural laws.

# TASK

List the medical drugs you have consumed over the past year, including the common drugs used for simple ailments like headaches and colds. Ask whether you could readily reduce or eliminate some of these drugs.

# PART 2

---

*Chastity*

# COMMUNITY

We propose to establish a school in the Lord's service, and we intend to lay down no rules that are harsh or hard to bear . . . Thus as each of us remains faithful to our calling as members of this school, we shall enjoy from God a sweetness of love that is beyond description. Let us remain as brothers until death parts us.

Benedict

# COMMUNITY

The first monks trekked out into the desert to be alone – indeed, the name 'monk' comes from the Greek word meaning 'solitary'. They intended to remain linked spiritually to the wider Church through prayer; and soon these hermits were receiving notes and messages from far distances, requesting them to intercede for the sick and the needy. But their intention was to remain physically cut off from the world.

Yet the human spirit is irredeemably communal; and soon hermits were coming together for worship and for friendship. They recognized that praying together is often far easier and far more effective than praying alone; and by agreeing to meet for worship at a certain time each day, they could impose on one another a strict discipline which ensured that they maintained a steady rhythm of prayer. They acknowledged too that conversation need not be an idle indulgence, but can be the breath of life at times of spiritual depression and exhaustion. And bread which is shared and eaten together feeds not just the body but the soul as well. Eventually Pachomius brought hermits together in a community, subject to a rule of life; and from then onwards the monastic movement has been mainly communal.

The monks in the desert were merely rediscovering a basic truth about humanity: that we are a social species, dependent emotionally as well as materially on one another. Since human beings first appeared on the planet, they have lived in groups; and the customs and mores of each society are in essence like a monastic rule, defining the pattern of life to which each individual must conform. In some groups the social solidarity has been so strong that individuals never speak of 'I' or 'me', but only of 'we' and 'us'. More commonly individuals have enjoyed personal property and freedom of choice, within a framework of social laws. And, despite wide variations in those laws, all traditional social groups have had one feature in common: that the group is sufficiently small for everyone to know each other personally.

Yet today in our large cities many people are in effect living like hermits – not through choice, but through force of circumstance. Whereas our ancestors used to work closely together, sowing crops or hunting animals, many of us work in large offices or factories where contact with others amounts to little more than snatched, inconsequential conversations. And many neighbourhoods are little more than aggregations of houses, with minimal social contact or common identity. The hermit in the desert was isolated by the physical remoteness of his cave; the modern hermit in the city is isolated by the spiritual remoteness of one person from another. As a consequence social customs and mores have grown increasingly weak, so that many people are confused and uncertain as to how they should behave. At its worst the isolation and confusion which people suffer lead to mindless violence, petty crime, drug abuse and even suicide – the ills which plague modern society.

With the exception of saving the natural environment, re-creating community is the most urgent and vital task which our civilization faces. Indeed these two challenges are closely connected: a strong sense of local community draws people together to care for their common environment. Thus, historically, monks have been good stewards of their land, caring for the soil, and planting trees and gardens. And the monastic example shows us the three essential elements of human community. The first is material. Human relationships cannot exist in a vacuum, but must be fostered by common practical concerns. As any monk will affirm, it is through cooking meals together in the monastery kitchen, or going out together on a chill autumn morning to dig potatoes, that friendships are forged. The second element is emotional. For all of us the primary emotional bond is with our families; but as monastic life shows, it is possible to create a profound sense of brotherhood amongst people who choose to come together – and who, like members of a family, remain loyal to one another in good and bad times alike. The third element is spiritual. The common prayer and worship of the monastery bind the monks together in spirit, and remind them constantly that, whenever conflict occurs amongst them, they must strive for forgiveness and reconciliation.

Every church congregation is also called to be a community; and it too must use these three elements to create a bond of love and faithfulness amongst its members. The most obvious element in church life is, of course, spiritual: coming together for worship is the main purpose of a church. Most congregations worship only once a week on Sunday; but clearly if some members were able to pray in common more often, the corporate life of the church would strengthen. In our mobile society church-going Christians have a distinct advantage when moving to a new neighbourhood, because they have an immediate circle of fresh friends in the local congregation. And it is a measure of the emotional health of a congregation that the members enjoy each other's company, chatting after worship, visiting each other's homes, and perhaps also going away together on pilgrimages. Most church buildings are both large and old, requiring continuous maintenance. As many congregations affirm, it is through working together to raise money for their building, and through doing the minor repairs themselves, that the warmest friendships are made – many profound theological discussions have taken place on medieval parapets while clearing leaves.

But the church does not, of course, exist for itself alone. Its members must seek to encourage a sense of community in the neighbourhood as a whole. There can no longer be the natural community of the ancient tribe or village, where by necessity and custom people lived and worked together. Yet this situation is not wholly new. Monasticism itself emerged at a similar period when traditional communities had broken down in the bustling cities of the Mediterranean; and the monasteries demonstrated it was possible to establish artificial communities, based on common beliefs and values. Equally in the modern world the most effective communities are those where people come together for a common purpose or to share a hobby. A sporting club, a local history society, a pressure group for conservation, or a dog-breeders' association can all become the context in which lasting friendships are formed. People of religious faith should be willing to play a full part in such groups, according to their own interests. And the insights which they have gained from religious community can prove extremely helpful in strengthening secular communities.

Throughout the medieval period the monasteries provided both the schools and the hospitals of Europe. From the seventeenth century these functions were shared by local churches, with many country clergy in England and elsewhere founding village schools and operating simple dispensaries from their own rectories. In our own century the state has largely taken over education and health care; and, until recently, most church people believed they no longer had a useful role to play in these spheres. But it is now clear that there are large and growing gaps in the state's provision, with many needs left unmet; and there is good reason to suppose that the state may eventually prove the wrong body to teach our young and heal our sick. In our own neighbourhoods we each have small opportunities to fill the gaps – and in doing so we are preparing ourselves for greater challenges to come. Setting aside the political arguments, we can be sure that there is no more effective means for a church or neighbourhood to become a community than for it to take charge of local health care and education: in both these spheres the spiritual, emotional and material elements of human community are perfectly balanced.

## TASK

Enumerate the various communities to which you belong. Ask to what extent they overlap and interact. And assess the spiritual and emotional importance of each community to you.

# FIDELITY

Wherever you are, always have God before your eyes. Whatever you do, do it according to the teachings of the gospel. And wherever you live, stay there, remaining faithful to those amongst whom God has placed you.

Anthony

# FIDELITY

When Pachomius formed the first monastic communities in the Egyptian desert, he built a fence around the outer edge of each monastery. Once a monk had entered a monastery and had been accepted into full membership, he could never again go outside the fence. Benedict laid down a similar rule, though he applied it less rigorously. In taking the vow of chastity, his monks were also promising to remain 'stable', staying within the same community for the rest of their lives. They were allowed to leave the monastery on errands or missions, with the permission of the abbot, but were not allowed to transfer their membership to another monastery.

Thus the monk must regard the community in which he lives as his family. At times he may find himself feeling intensely angry or irritated at some of the other monks. And inevitably, as in any family, there are furious rows and disputes within a monastery. But the monk cannot walk out, hoping to find more congenial and sympathetic company in another monastery. Rather he must strive to love the people he dislikes, and to make peace whenever harsh words have been exchanged. As Benedict taught, a monk must accept the other members of the community as if they were brothers by blood. And if a monk is ever tempted to escape from his monastic family, he should remind himself that he would find the same irritations and the same disputes in any other monastery – or indeed in any ordinary family.

Benedict described his monasteries as schools for sinners. When a person lives alone, he can imagine himself to be kind and loving towards others, free of all malice. But when he joins a community, and must encounter day after day the same group of people, he can find that all manner of negative emotions, which had lain dormant. erupt within his heart. He is jealous of the greater talents or higher status of another monk. He feels resentful about the cell he is allocated or the work he is required to do, believing that others enjoy special privileges. He is overwhelmed by intense annoyance at the personal habits of his brethren, harbouring thoughts of vengeance towards the monk who clicks his false teeth in chapel or takes the largest helping at dinner. He is contemptuous towards the vulgar tastes and humour of his humbler brethren, snobbishly spurning their overtures of friendship. And, despite his commitment to humble service, he is ambitious to achieve high office within the monastery, and thus assert his will over others. Benedict, and every other monastic leader, has recognized that such attitudes bubble within the heart of any human being who seeks to live in close proximity with others. And only by remaining unquestioningly faithful to the brethren with whom God has placed him, can the monk learn to transform jealousy into admiration, anger into gentleness, and hatred into love.

When a man and a woman make marriage vows, they too commit themselves to remain 'stable' for the rest of their lives. Unlike Benedictine monks, they can move house whenever they wish; but like monks they must be faithful to one another 'till death us do part'. And, as in a monastery, so in any marriage there are negative emotions of anger, jealousy, irritation, resentment and perhaps at times a degree of hatred. There are few husbands and wives who have not in dark moments been tempted to abandon the partnership, imagining that life would be so much more tranquil and pleasant on one's own – or with a different partner. And the temptation can be accompanied by the most intense sexual desire, in which another member of the opposite sex seems infinitely more attractive than one's spouse. But if the couple stay firm in their mutual fidelity, then marriage too becomes a school in which sinners become holy.

Much as we would wish it otherwise, the battle for stability lies at the heart of marriage. Like most other higher species, the human being instinctively seeks marriage. The purpose of this marital instinct is to provide a secure context in which to rear young, and also to create a social group which can cooperate in

foraging and hunting for food. Yet like almost every other species, the human being takes an instinctive pleasure in courtship,
in which a sexual mate is sought. And the enjoyment of courtship
does not cease as soon as a partner is found, but continues, in
increasingly muted form, until old age. As human societies have
found since the dawn of history, the conflict can only be resolved
through husband and wife taking vows, in which they promise
to remain sexually and emotionally faithful. Once made these
vows must never be questioned or doubted, but should be
regarded as fixed and unshakeable. In this way the couple leave
themselves with no choice but to continue seeking peace and
good will within the home – and in seeking it, they will find it.

Visitors to monasteries are often struck by the apparent lack of
communication between the monks. Even during the recreation
period each evening, when conversation is encouraged, a few
words and grunts seem sufficient to release a gale of laughter.
Similarly couples who have been happily married for three or
four decades seem rarely ever to finish sentences. Yet the sparse-
ness of talk, far from signifying that love is dead, is an indication
of profound mutual understanding – which is the reward of
fidelity. Through working so hard and for so long in learning
to love one another, they know every nook and cranny of each
other's personality. So even a look of the eye or a gesture of the
hand can be enough to express quite complex emotions, while
thoughts and ideas may be shared with a few simple phrases that
would make no sense to a stranger. A relationship which has
sailed through storms and over rocks to achieve such calm and
easy sympathy is truly holy.

The calling to fidelity does not, however, apply only to monks
and spouses: it extends to all friendships and to villages and
neighbourhoods. Today in most Western countries people move
house on average every five or ten years. And at each move they
sever the relationships they have formed with neighbours and
colleagues. As the years pass people can become increasingly
reluctant to forge new bonds, insulating themselves from the
pain of breaking the bonds at the next move. The consequence
is that many of us have no close friends outside the home, but
instead have a growing list of former acquaintances with whom

we exchange Christmas cards. Not only does this breed loneliness and depression, but also places excessive emotional demands on marriage as the sole source of emotional fulfilment – and paradoxically increases the likelihood of a marriage breaking up, under the weight of these demands.

Some moves are forced by economic necessity, or are impelled by a clear sense of calling. But where economic advancement is the main motivation, we should question whether the material benefits exceed the emotional and spiritual costs. And in reaching a decision, we should seek the advice of friends, so that even if moving proves right, trust and fellowship have not been betrayed. Moreover, wherever possible, good friendships formed in earlier phases of life should be sustained by more than a cursory card each year: visits to each other's homes, perhaps holidays together, and prayer for one another, can serve to extend the boundaries of community over hundreds of miles. The example to follow in such circumstances is not the Benedictine monastery, but the Jesuits and similar religious orders, which over recent centuries have sent missionaries across the world. They have maintained spiritual stability and fidelity through unflagging intercession for one another, and through being willing to travel huge distances to come together for meetings. Loyal friendship is a jewel for which sore feet are a small price.

## TASK

Write to two or three friends on your Christmas card list, with whom you would like to sustain a closer friendship. Suggest that you meet, perhaps inviting them to stay at your house.

# CELIBACY

Virginity is not a physical condition, but a spiritual state. All may acquire this state, if they love God with their whole selves.

Teresa

# CELIBACY

For the monk the vow of chastity requires, of course, lifelong celibacy – or 'perpetual virginity' as it was often described. Some monks have believed celibacy is a higher calling than that of marriage. And at one point in the early centuries so many Christians embraced celibacy that there was anxiety that the Church would die out. But most monks have accepted celibacy as their particular vocation, while recognizing that the challenge of married life can be no less rigorous.

Today celibacy is commonly regarded as unhealthy and unnatural. We are bombarded with images on television and in magazines that associate physical sexual expression with personal fulfilment. And under the influence of Freudian psychology – or, rather, a bowdlerized version of Freud's thought – we have come to believe that an active sexual partnership is vital for emotional and physical well-being. Thus the man or woman who remains single is looked upon with pity, as someone who must either be too repressed to perform sexually, or too unattractive to find a mate. And the person who openly declares a preference for celibacy is assumed to be psychologically unhinged – or merely making virtue out of necessity.

Yet celibacy, far from being unnatural, is actually the most common sexual condition. For the first fifteen, twenty or more years of life both boys and girls are denied full sexual expression, even though after puberty the sexual urge may be very strong. And in many primitive tribes young men remain single until the age of twenty-five or thirty, in order to be warriors defending the tribal lands. Then when one partner in a marriage has died, the surviving partner usually remains single until their own death. Thus most people are sexually active for only a third or a half of their life-span. Moreover anthropologists suggest that homo sapiens developed from a baboon-like creature, in which only the most intelligent and dextrous males were allowed to mate, while the majority of males acted as hunters, risking their lives to get meat for the top males and their many wives to eat. Thus the very evolution of our species depended upon celibacy.

As monastic writers have always taught, celibacy is not denial of sexuality, but rather a particular way of channelling it. Aelred, the great abbot of Rievaulx, spoke of the 'spiritual embrace' and the 'spiritual kiss' which two monks or nuns can exchange, which is both erotic and pure. Aelred encouraged his monks to recognize that all human relationships have a sexual element, which in close friendships can become extremely intense. If this sexual element is denied full physical expression, its energy is directed towards the spiritual dimension of the friendship, enabling two monks to become true brothers on the road to holiness. Aelred fully recognized the temptations inherent in such friendships – and he himself was a homosexual by inclination – but believed that monks who had taken a solemn vow of celibacy could trust in each other's strength to resist the temptation.

Celibacy can thus enrich human relationships, strengthening spiritual bonds. It also allows a breadth of friendship which for most married couples is impossible. Marriage is to some degree exclusive, not only sexually but also emotionally: through sharing a bed and a home, and through the daily demands of family life, married couples have only limited love and attention to give to others. Moreover many well-matched couples receive such a high degree of emotional satisfaction from one another, that they feel little desire or need for friendships outside. The celibate person, by contrast, depends on a circle of friends to sustain him emotionally. And he has both time and mental space to devote to those friends.

Aelred's older contemporary, Anselm, composed prayers of great warmth and intimacy, and at times quite explicit eroticism, to various saints and biblical figures. And over the centuries numerous other monks and nuns have discovered for themselves the same style of prayer, in which both the body and the soul are directed towards God. Again the married couple, whose sexual needs are satisfied through physical intimacy, can have only a small taste of such prayer. But for the celibate natural sexual desire can over time be transmuted into spiritual desire for God.

In the first churches, described in the New Testament, there were groups of widows that played a central role in the spiritual and social ministry of the Christian community. These widows were committed to remaining celibate for the rest of their lives, so that they could devote themselves entirely to prayer and service. Such groups were the models of the early convents, situated in towns and villages throughout the Roman Empire, where the sick were cared for and travellers welcomed. Similarly today in every parish there are single people – particularly widows – who form the spiritual heart of both the church and the neighbourhood. They are regular and devout in their worship; they raise money, and give generously from their own funds, for charity; they visit the sick and the bereaved, giving both spiritual succour and practical help; and their homes are always open, where they offer refreshment and friendly conversation to anyone who calls. And they ask for neither public recognition nor private gratitude.

The discipline of celibacy is not, however, confined to those who are single. On the contrary, there is one respect in which it should apply to us all – and this application is increasingly important. Today, when the majority of women have paid jobs, men and women frequently find themselves as colleagues at work; and friendships naturally spring up between them. But if the men and the women are already married, there is the obvious danger that such friendships will lead to adultery. Thus understandably relationships between the sexes in the office and factory are often viewed with great suspicion. Yet if the men and the women appreciate and accept the discipline of celibacy within the friendship, the danger melts away. They can acknowledge and even enjoy the sexual attraction between them, allowing it to strengthen their emotional and spiritual bond. By this means their respective marriages are not only secure, but may even be improved – since all good human relationships enrich one another.

## TASK

Reflect honestly on your sexual feelings, asking to what extent they infuse your relationships with both men and women. Try to assess whether your sexual feelings find fulfilment in these relationships, without direct physical expression.

# SEX

Sexuality throws no light on love. But only through love can we learn to understand our sexual feelings.

                                                        Aelred

# SEX

Monks are no less susceptible to the sin of envy than the rest of us. So when they look over the monastery wall at their married friends in the world, they are inclined to imagine that every couple enjoys a passionate and pleasurable sexual relationship. Yet equally many married people look enviously towards the monastery, jealous of the freedom from sexual anxiety which monks appear to enjoy.

Some couples are justly the objects of monastic envy, achieving throughout their married life a high level of sexual fulfilment. They make love frequently, and almost invariably they satisfy one another. But for many couples sex is a source of frequent disappointment, and even bitter misery. As many as a half of all men are to some degree impotent, so are often unable to sustain intercourse for any length of time before reaching a climax. And an equal number of women are either permanently or intermittently frigid, recoiling from sexual intercourse. Thus in only a minority of couples can both partners consistently give each other satisfaction. And in modern Western culture, which is so obsessed with sexual performance, many couples regard this inability as a harsh failure.

The primary biological purpose of sex is, of course, procreation. Yet the sexual ability needed to conceive a child is very limited, so that even couples for whom sex is perfunctory and passionless can produce a family. Besides, in a world already grossly overpopulated, we need to constrain, not encourage, the biological imperative. Indeed some anthropologists have suggested that the high incidence of sexual impotence in modern society is Nature's way of limiting the population.

Sex does, however, have a secondary natural function, which is shared by a number of higher animal species: to strengthen the bond between male and female. Sexual attraction, and the pleasure of sexual contact, helps to create and sustain the partnership between husband and wife on which the human social order is founded. Yet, as with other species, this sexual bonding does not depend on intercourse itself. A man and woman can derive great sexual pleasure simply by looking at each other, and being in each other's company. And quite limited sexual activity, such as embracing and kissing, can for many people prove very satisfying. Indeed sexual attraction is often more durable if there is some restraint in its physical expression.

Such restraint is perfectly natural. The human body is designed to survive twenty or forty years after the capacity for child-bearing has ceased. So throughout this latter period of life full intercourse has lost its biological purpose. Moreover as the body ages, its sexual potency is bound to decline. Yet the social and emotional purpose of marriage remains. Thus a quieter and more peaceful sexual relationship, in which the fire of youthful passion becomes a warm, steady glow, is quite normal. Seen in this light the widespread inability of couples to achieve satisfactory intercourse is not a mark of failure, but part of the natural development of human sexuality after the years of procreation. Indeed, as researchers in this field have repeatedly found, couples who are content with limited physical expression, rather than resenting their lack of potency, enjoy the happiest and most harmonious marriages.

While a monk depends on no one and disappoints no one in deciding to be celibate, married couples must agree on how to conduct their sexual relationship. From the earliest decades of the Christian Church couples were encouraged to abstain from intercourse, either permanently or for a period. This was not, as is sometimes supposed, because sex was regarded as sinful or dirty. On the contrary the church inherited from the Hebrew tradition a robust and wholesome attitude to sexual pleasure. Rather the early Christian teachers realized that for many people intercourse is a source of fear and even distress, and hence a spiritual destruction. Abstaining from intercourse would bring spiritual peace, and, paradoxically, strengthen the sexual bond between husband and wife, since they could enjoy limited sexual contact without anxiety. The monasteries took this teaching to its logical conclusion, inviting couples whose children had grown up to take monastic vows. This practice was especially common in the Celtic church of Britain and Ireland, where monks and nuns often lived side by side: many mixed monasteries were filled with married couples who remained spiritually committed to one another, but physically celibate.

A married couple who embrace celibacy, or who at least regard physical sex as relatively unimportant, will come to find that sex is an element in all their relationships – as monks and nuns have always found. A young couple, in the first flush of romantic passion, naturally focus all their sexual feelings on one another, and thus regard sex as exclusive. But as sexual fire turns to peaceful glow, husband and wife come to experience a degree of physical, as well as emotional, attraction towards all their friends. Thus their marital bond becomes inclusive, drawing in others to share their love – and enables their marriage to be a source of strength to others, and their home a place of warm welcome.

Monastic teachers, such as Aelred of Rievaulx, have applied the same wisdom to the strange human phenomenon of homosexuality. No one knows why around one tenth of the population should defy the biological purpose of sex, feeling the same physical attraction to members of their own sex as heterosexuals feel towards the opposite sex. It may be a form of arrested psychological development, or due to some chemical imbalance within the body, or perhaps it is another of Nature's methods of limiting the population – as other species abort or eat their young when their numbers within an area grow too large. But, whatever the cause, it is a condition which is permanent and, except in very rare instances, cannot be altered by any form of therapy. Homosexuals tend to suffer greater anxiety about physical sex than do heterosexuals, partly because of the moral stigma attaching to their activities, and partly because of the greater difficulty which many homosexuals experience in forming stable sexual partnerships. However, as Aelred taught, once the homosexual is no longer seeking physical sex, he experiences the same liberation as the heterosexual: he can recognize and enjoy the sexual element in all his friendships, with both men and women. Indeed such an attitude to sexuality breaks down the barrier, which has been the cause of so much intolerance and even persecution, between homosexual and heterosexual, since for both sex is the servant of love.

# TASK

If you are married, ask your spouse whether he or she is satisfied with your sexual relationship. And ask yourself the same question. Discuss as openly as possible both the sources of sexual satisfaction between you, and also any causes of frustration. Do not be afraid to ask for more sexual contact or for less – and even to suggest a period of celibacy.

# HONESTY

Let each one honestly make known his needs to his brethren, that they may minister to him. And each one should honestly love and care for his brethren, as a mother loves and cares for her son.

Francis

# HONESTY

Many monasteries periodically hold a 'chapter of faults'. The form varies from one community to another, but the essence is the same. The monks apologize for the ways in which they have wronged others, or failed to live up to the monastic ideals. Often the faults are quite trivial, such as a monk forgetting to take his turn washing up the dishes after a meal – though, as in a family, such incidents can generate intense emotions. But occasionally a serious misdemeanour is revealed, such as the cellarer of the monastery abusing his position by taking extra food for himself, or two monks exchanging blows in the course of an argument. This meeting is not a personal confession, at which absolution is given; that must wait for the privacy of the confessional. Rather it is an opportunity for the brethren to make peace with one another, and also to explore ways in which the monastery as a whole may be falling short.

Monastic teachers such as Aelred have encouraged an even greater degree of honesty between friends within the monastery. Love, he taught, is an illusion unless there is truth, since we can only love what we know. And if we are to make progress in our spiritual journey, we need friends in whom we can confide, revealing our own joys and sorrows, hopes and anxieties – and listening to the secrets of their hearts. Such honest friendship is not always easy and pleasant. To Aelred the test of a true friend is that he is willing to criticize you, pointing out your faults and failures, and then to stand by you even if your initial response to criticism is anger and antagonism. Thus friends should be completely open with each other, making no attempt to cover over their sinfulness, in order both to affirm one another's virtues and correct one another's faults.

A marriage needs no chapter of faults for husband and wife

to become aware of each other's shortcomings. A boy and a girl when they first fall in love imagine each other to be perfect; and while they only go out together, enjoying parties and holidays, this happy illusion persists. But once they set up home together, encountering one another in the cold light of early morning and over piles of dirty dishes and clothes, she can soon be driven to distraction by his untidiness and laziness in the house, and he can be maddened by her extravagance and petty jealousies. Yet if husband and wife know only too intimately one another's sins, they need, like monks in the monastery, to learn to apologize and make amends. The husband must strive to see himself as his wife sees him, and the wife look at herself through his eyes; in this way each will want to say sorry, and to learn better habits and attitudes.

But even in the most honest marriages it is rare for husband and wife to enjoy perfect mutual understanding. Thus we need other partners to share the journey. Sadly we do not have, like the monks, a close community from which to find spiritual partners. But so important is our need for true friends that we need to seek out a church, or other social institutions which bring people together, where we can expect to meet people of similar outlook. There is no need for us to be diffident or reticent in seeking friends, since everyone shares the same need. And as a relationship forms, so we should positively invite criticism and ask advice, to indicate that such honesty is what we desire.

While Aelred sung so passionately of the blessings of friendship, and while monks through the ages can testify to the value of the chapter of faults, monastic teachers have been equally forceful in pointing out the dangers of excessive honesty, that goes beyond what we can bear. Every sin or failing revealed within the chapter of faults is thereafter public knowledge; so the sinner has to live not only with the painful truth about himself, but the fact that everyone around him is aware of that truth. For someone whose confidence and self-esteem is already weak this can prove a terrifying strain. Moreover, if the meetings are extremely tense, the emotional temperature of the monastery can rise rapidly, so that monks find themselves unable to relax and rest. With personal friendships, where the level of communication is even deeper, the problems can seem even more acute. As Aelred himself found, the advice and criticism which one friend offers to another can be so hurtful that it brings self-hatred and despair, not spiritual progress. Worse still, where spiritual insights are being shared, words are frequently quite inadequate as a means of communication, so bitter misunderstanding can easily occur.

Such difficulties are familiar to almost every married couple. Since all pretences soon break down in the home, husband and wife feel vulnerable and exposed to one another. And if a note of contempt or disparagement is sounded, as one comes to perceive the shortcomings of the other, love can soon be mixed with fear and self-pity. Every husband and wife have found themselves at times feeling impatient and annoyed with each other, so that words of advice and criticism, which may appear constructive and well-intended, are in truth vehicles of anger. And there are few marriages that have not experienced periods of profound misunderstanding where words fail to convey thoughts and emotions, so that each partner feels isolated and lonely within the home.

Monastic literature abounds with reference to the importance of confidentiality within personal relationships: that the deeper and more honest – and hence the more spiritually creative – relationships become, the more vital it is that the inner truths people learn about each other are treated as sacred and inviolable. At the chapter of faults there is a double obligation of confidentiality: not only are monks forbidden to reveal what has been said to those not at the chapter; they are not allowed even to discuss afterwards the contents of the meeting between themselves. Thus each monk can speak freely at the chapter, knowing that whatever he says will never be referred to again. Similarly within personal friendships an individual should never talk about what he has learned in private conversations to anyone else.

Yet confidentiality goes further than simply holding one's counsel. It implies that people should have confidence in one another, that whatever they say to each other will never be abused as a vehicle of power or malice. It is a dire sin within a monastery for a monk, even in the heat of anger, to refer disdainfully to something that another monk has vouchsafed in trust. Similarly within a marriage, or amongst personal friends, it is a gross abuse of trust to pass any kind of barbed remark based on intimate knowledge.

Such marital confidence can only build up slowly, through being tested in small ways before greater truths are shared. In recent decades many people have tried to break out of their isolation by attending courses in which they are encouraged to talk with absolute frankness to complete strangers. Equally in neighbourhoods and workplaces – and churches – people are often eager to establish intimate relationships after only a few meetings. Yet an instant friendship can cause lasting damage if confidences are betrayed, since it leaves a scar of distrust, making it more difficult to make new friends in the future. Indeed there are horrific numbers of people who are so wounded by past betrayals that they are now incapable of intimacy – and are thus permanent emotional cripples. Honesty between people requires patience and caution – which is why new monks must serve three or more years as novices, before being allowed to the chapter of faults.

## TASK

Ask whether there is someone in your life from whom you can take frank and honest criticism, without it threatening the relationship. If there is no such person, ask whether you have the courage to seek such a person – whether a professional such as a priest or counsellor, or a close friend who acts as confidant.

# FORGIVENESS

If you have wronged someone by abusing him or cursing him or accusing him falsely, go and apologize as quickly as possible. And the one who has been wronged should in his turn be willing to forgive you without wrangling.

Augustine

# FORGIVENESS

Benedict taught that if one monk feels himself wronged by another monk, he should have the courage to speak to him. Through discussion they should strive to reach a common view of what has been happening; and if they cannot achieve this common view by themselves, they should ask a third monk to listen to both explanations, to ask questions, and then to give a judgement. If at the end of this process it is decided that wrong has been committed, the wrongdoer should give an unconditional apology – and the victim offer unconditional forgiveness. If an apology is not given, and forgiveness not granted, a moral and spiritual barrier will have been erected between the two individuals. And if many such barriers are erected within the monastery, people will begin to divide into factions, as those who feel themselves wronged forge alliances against those whom they see as wrongdoers. Eventually the community itself will be threatened.

This pattern of apology and forgiveness is manifestly vital, both for good personal relationships, and for the integrity of any group. Yet apology and forgiveness are often horrendously difficult. In order to apologize a person must first admit to himself that he is wrong; and so stubborn is our moral and spiritual pride, that we will often fiercely resist such an admission, even within the privacy of our own heads. Indeed all of us have experienced the internal tussle in which conscience says that we have done wrong, and pride says the opposite. But even if pride loses this first battle, it then retreats to fight another even bloodier battle – against admitting the wrong openly to the victim. Rather than apologize unconditionally, we find all manner of excuses and qualifications, many of which are intended to cast blame on the victim himself. Whenever we hear ourselves saying, 'I'm sorry, but . . .' we can be sure that pride has undermined the apology.

If apologizing is hard, forgiving can be an epic moral struggle. As Augustine taught, to forgive is to recognize that the same moral and spiritual evil, which caused another to commit wrong, is present within one's own heart. And, to show the dimensions of this recognition, he asked his monks to think of the worst sin they could imagine anyone committing – and then to look inside themselves to discover the capacity to commit that sin themselves. Thus forgiving someone who has done wrong is to put ourselves on their moral level. In the process we are forced to give up the one compensation – the one reward – of being the victim of wrong, that we are morally superior to the wrong-doer. Not surprisingly Augustine warned his monks that pride struggles even more furiously against forgiving than against apologizing.

There is a second reward that must also be given up when we offer forgiveness. Many of us as children learn that being a victim of the wrongs of others both brings sympathy, and enables us to avoid taking responsibility for our situation – since the victim is powerless. Thus we can easily acquire the social and psychological technique of making ourselves victims whenever life becomes unduly difficult and demanding. And the emotion of the victim, resentment at other's wrongs, become habitual, and is even experienced as comfortable. To forgive is to cease being the impotent victim, and to become instead an equal partner of the person apologizing, jointly responsible for maintaining mutual harmony. To many of us such responsibility is quite terrifying.

The closer the relationship, the more difficult apologizing and forgiving becomes. Thus marriages in particular can harbour whole fleets of grudges, dating back over many years. These may relate to specific events, such as the husband resenting his wife's failure to support him when he was offered promotion in another part of the country, because she did not want to move house; or the wife remembering with unquenchable bitterness a brief affair her husband had twenty years ago. More usually, however, the resentments are general, such as one partner resenting the other's lack of physical affection, or persistent mutual grudges about how money is spent, each regarding the other's expenditure as extravagant. Marriages can become set in a rigid pattern of unforgiveness, in which neither can admit fault nor offer reconciliation. And while in so many respects a marriage may be loving and creative, grudges and resentments can slowly and insidiously undermine it.

Benedict's rule, that a third monk be appointed to reconcile rifts between monks, applies beyond the monastery to marriage and to all friendships. When our pride is under threat, we are often deafened to the meaning of what others are saying. So we may not be able to hear the anguish of someone who feels we are doing them wrong; and as victims we may shut our minds to the sincere efforts of a wrongdoer to apologize. A third person can act as interpreter, putting the points that we need to hear in ways that skirt round our pride. This is especially true in marriage, when too easily husband and wife can cease to respond to each other's thoughts and feelings. But a confidant need not only be sought in times of crisis, where anger is high and resentment is deep. In no relationship is communication perfect, and in every relationship there are small misunderstandings, and trivial acts of selfishness which, if left unattended, can grow into weeds that choke the spirit of love. If each of us has someone we can talk to intimately about matters of deep concern, these weeds can be uprooted as soon as they sprout.

When we anticipate making an apology, it can seem a dire and fearsome prospect. And when we realize that we must offer forgiveness, we can dread letting go our moral superiority. Yet in the event apology and forgiveness are moments of profound joy. And a relationship, which has been damaged and even broken, is restored to even greater strength when both sides cast aside pride and seek reconciliation. As Augustine speculated, sin can be perceived as part of the divine plan, in order to bring God's healing grace to the hearts of men and women.

# TASK

Ask whether there is anyone with whom, for whatever reason, you are not reconciled. Then reflect on the degree to which you may be at fault for the rift. Visit or write to the person, apologizing to them for what you have done wrong, without reservation and without expecting an apology in return.

# CHILDREN

Children are God's apostles, day by day sent forth to inspire in people's hearts love, hope and peace.

Francis

# CHILDREN

Most of the original monasteries of Britain and Ireland in the fifth and sixth centuries were also schools. Those monks who were educated themselves acted as teachers, passing on to their pupils the rare skills of reading and writing, as well as instilling the Christian faith and its moral values. Thus the typical Celtic monastery had as many children and young people as professed monks. And these monastic schools were a major tool of evangelism, since local chiefs often sent their sons there – and when these sons themselves became chiefs, they converted the tribes under their rule to the new faith. Iltut, for example, was largely responsible for the conversion of Wales to Christianity through his extraordinary monastic school on the Glamorgan coast: he attracted aristocratic offspring from the entire country, some of whom became rulers, while others became monastic evangelists themselves, including St David himself.

Benedictine monasteries have an even greater reputation for education, which continues to this day. Many of the finest schools in Europe and America are within Benedictine communities, or were founded by Benedictines and then became secular establishments at the Reformation. In addition children could be offered as 'oblates' to the monastry, which would be entirely responsible for their upbringing; before the days of state welfare this was a common method of looking after orphans. The boys in the monastery followed a diluted form of the monastic rule, attending some of the services, eating with the monks, and sharing in the physical labour. An incidental virtue of monastic education was that the Benedictines, who were often pioneers in new agricultural methods, were able to spread their ideas far and wide through the young men who emerged from their schools.

The presence of children within a monastery help to keep the monks good-humoured and open-minded – they make the monastery more natural in its attitudes and behaviour. And, of course, children bring the same benefits to a family. Yet parents who feel called to live a holy life in the modern world find themselves in a dilemma over how to bring up their children. Traditional monastic ideas of holiness are today regarded as odd, even eccentric, so a child raised by parents committed to such ideas will experience a clash between the values at home and the values at school and in the neighbourhood. And since children naturally wish to win both the approval of adults and the friendship of peers, this clash can be acutely painful and confusing, as the child strives unsuccessfully to please parents, teachers and other children. The parents for their part feel under increasing pressure to give way, allowing their child to conform with his friends. At first tension may focus on trivial matters, such as the volume of chocolate consumed – or, indeed, whether to permit chocolate at all – and the amount of pocket money given. But as the years pass so wider questions are posed about diet, stewardship of income and wealth, sexuality, hospitality, attitudes to personal health – the whole range of issues where the monastic view of holiness is at odds with the dominant values of contemporary culture.

There is no way that parents can spare their children the pain and confusion of this moral and religious clash. If the parents try to ease matters by bowing to pressure, the confusion is actually worsened: the child senses that the parents are not being true to themselves, which both reduces the child's trust in his parents, and gives the impression to the child that hypocrisy and cowardice are morally acceptable. The right course is for the parents to remain loyal to their own values, and, to the limits of their parental authority, impose these values on their children. This will inevitably lead to arguments, which must be calmly endured. Yet as the child becomes a teenager he will have learnt to respect his parents' courage, even when he disagrees with them. And, though he may eventually reject many practical aspects of his parents' way of life, he will probably carry into adulthood four essential elements of holiness.

The first is fidelity. The importance of faithfulness in personal relationships can only be learnt by example. Thus children whose parents not only remain married, but who continue to be open and responsive towards each other through their married life, are far more likely to form stable, responsive partnerships themselves. Equally, children of parents who retain a close circle of friends, to whom they remain loyal in bad times as well as good, will see for themselves the comfort and strength such loyalty brings – and will want to find it for themselves.

The second element is forgiveness. If we find it difficult to apologize to a fellow adult, we are doubly reluctant to apologize to a child – especially our own. Thus when we wrongly become angry with a child, and even deliver a spank out of irritation rather than as a proper act of discipline, we do not readily say 'sorry' and seek forgiveness. Equally when we selfishly put our own desires before those of a child, we rarely admit it. Yet if parents can bring themselves to apologize to their children, the effects can be miraculous: the child is usually very quick to forgive, and the bond of love between parent and child is wonderfully strengthened. Moreover, children that have been raised by parents who readily give and receive forgiveness, will carry that practice into their own adult relationships – and eventually into their own behaviour as parents.

The third element is hope. Children who have been brought up by parents committed to the Christian ideal will not necessarily remain Christian in adulthood; but they will very probably remain idealistic, aspiring to live by values that go beyond their own wants and needs. Equally many of the finest Christians were not raised in Christian households, but nonetheless had parents with strong moral values and ideals – even secular ideals, such as those of socialism and communism. Thus parents following the way of holiness will pass on to their children that most precious and fragile gift of hope: hope that sin and evil can be transformed into goodness and love, and hope that the miseries of this world can be turned into joy.

The fourth element is discipline. Children naturally want clear and consistent guidance, in which both good and bad behaviour are spelled out. Only if parents clearly and consistently guide their own behaviour can they offer such guidance to their children. Parents who are seeking to follow the way of holiness must of necessity impose quite strict discipline on themselves, so they will have little difficulty in imposing it on their children. And if holiness also includes gentleness and patience, the parental discipline will be such as to encourage rather than stifle the innate goodness of the children. As they imbibe their parents' values, so the external disciplines will become self-discipline – an essential ingredient of a creative and successful adulthood, in which hopes and visions can be turned into reality.

Just as the children of the Celtic monastery became evangelists of the Christian faith, so our children can be our most effective witnesses. The best testimony for the way of holiness is a balanced, peaceful and purposeful teenager. Of course our children today are subject to numerous influences, many of which are corrupt, so that parents should not paralyse themselves with self-blame when their offspring go astray and become morose and depressed. On the contrary, the times of anxiety and even crisis within the family are the greatest tests of our call to holiness. Nor should we worry if our children reject our own religious beliefs – after all, beliefs are only man-made formulations of divine mysteries far beyond our grasp. But if we can maintain a good and honest relationship with our growing children, and if they for their part are trustworthy, forgiving, hopeful and self-disciplined, our spiritual journey has been vindicated. And others will wonder at how such a happy result has been achieved.

# TASK

If you are a parent or a teacher, or in any other role have charge
of children, reflect on your pattern of discipline. Write down
the basic values and forms of behaviour you wish to encourage,
and ask whether you are consistent in offering such encouragement.

# AGE

To know how to grow old is the master work of wisdom, and one of the most difficult chapters in the book of life.

Francis

# AGE

A monk never retires. The work of prayer can continue until the breath leaves his body – and continues thereafter around the throne of God. But even his service to others is likely to carry on until within a few weeks, or even days and hours, of his death. The monastery has useful tasks for people at every stage of life. The young monks do the heavier manual jobs, as well as run the school and go out preaching. The older monks perform the lighter jobs, including housework, take small classes of children, and act as confessors and counsellors, both to their brethren and to lay people from outside. Some older monks may choose to become hermits, living in a hut some distance from the monastery; but even there they are likely to be sought out for advice and counsel. In the Coptic communities of Egypt and Ethiopia there is a sharp division of leadership between old and young, to ensure that the older monks' wisdom and the younger monks' vision are both harnessed in the service of the monastery. The abbot and the other officers are chosen from amongst the younger monks; and they take practical decisions, managing the work and the resources of the monastery. The spiritual directors, however, are chosen from amongst the older monks; and they not only counsel individual monks, but also have charge of the community's discipline and worship.

The monastic attitude to old age is no different to that of traditional tribal societies. The old men and women in the tribe continued to sow seed, to feed livestock and to cook, leaving the younger ones to dig the soil, go hunting and grind the corn. And grandfathers and grandmothers played with the small children while the parents were working, and told the ancient myths and legends of the tribe to the bigger children. The old also had time to nurse the sick – until they themselves needed nursing. Tribal government made full use of the experience of the old men, allowing no decision to be made until they had offered advice.

Modern society, by contrast, has little or no place for the elderly. Since the Industrial Revolution in the early nineteenth century most people have worked away from home in factories and offices; so an old person cannot gradually reduce the hours he works and change to lighter tasks, but must retire completely. Equally education and health care also take place away from home in schools and hospitals, where professional staff have charge; so the elderly are excluded from these spheres also. Worse still, as people move many hundreds of miles in search of employment, most grandparents live far away from their grandchildren, depriving them of any role in their upbringing. And as for modern government, there is little respect for the wisdom of experience. Thus when a person reaches the age of retirement, he is discarded from all productive activity, condemned to pass his remaining years in idle amusements.

Yet the weakness of communal bonds in the modern town or village, and thence the loneliness and isolation which many people suffer, leave the elderly an invaluable task to perform – if only the rest of us would give encouragement and affirmation. Anyone familiar with monastic life can testify that the older monks are the glue which holds the community together. Similarly within a neighbourhood the elderly can potentially turn a mere aggregation of houses into a community. In the first place they have time to talk, and so become channels of communication. They may visit those who are sick and those suffering depression or any other kind of mental disorder – of which there are far more than we commonly imagine. They may befriend the children in the area; and if a child is falling behind in learning to read or do sums, an elderly person may offer extra practice after school. They may organize local societies, bringing together people with common interests, and also play a major part in putting on social events. And they may even edit and publish a neighbourhood magazine, to keep people in touch with local events.

There are villagers and neighbourhoods within towns where

the elderly succeed in creating community in this fashion. Usually one or two popular and brave elderly people have pioneered this work, and others have followed; and even when the pioneers die, a strong tradition has been established which allows it to continue. But in most villages and neighbourhoods the elderly feel too diffident to create community, and they receive little or no encouragement from others. Moreover too many old people are themselves trapped in the psychology of retirement, refusing to consider working for the locality without payment – and hence allowing themselves to remain useless. The talents and wisdom of the elderly will only be released if they themselves cease to regard retirement as the end of work – and if the rest of us realize how much we need them.

Age brings particular challenges, and potential problems, within marriage. When the children leave home, husband and wife are alone for the first time in about a quarter of a century. Some couples find themselves falling in love anew, enjoying each other's company and acquiring new zest and sparkle in their sexual relationship. Other couples, however, realize that through the long years of child-rearing they have ceased to communicate, and gradually drifted apart; so now, as they face each other across the dining table, they have nothing to say. They may seek to revive the partnership by going on more holidays together, pursuing common hobbies and interests, and sharing more closely in running the home and garden. And to their surprise and joy, they may rediscover the love which first drew them together. But, despite their best efforts, they may be forced to conclude that their marriage is a source of mutual oppression, in which each feels stifled by the needs and expectations of the other.

This conclusion should not, however, be regarded as a failure; rather it is an opportunity. We have all observed people who seem to flourish after their spouse has died, growing in confidence and energy. A widow in her mid-sixties may start travelling the world, take quite demanding courses at the local college, or become a stimulating and amusing public speaker; and when asked why she did none of these things earlier, she replies that her husband would not have liked it. Or more simply she finds great satisfaction in taking over tasks that her husband used to do, such as looking after the household finances or tending the garden. And widowers equally may blossom, even becoming superb cooks now that they are free to go into the kitchen. Yet when we see widows and widowers thriving in this way, we cannot help regretting that they could not have enjoyed the same opportunities while their spouses were alive.

All of us who are married should, when we reach late middle age, review our partnership, looking for the ways in which quite unconsciously we may inhibit one another. Then we must be generous in trying to liberate each other. In some monasteries every few years the monks conduct a radical reassessment of how the work of the community is distributed, to ensure the people's gifts are not wasted; and at the end of the review some tasks are reallocated, to allow monks to develop new talents. Similarly a marriage partnership can find new vigour if some jobs are swapped – the wife can take over the finances, the husband starts cooking and cleaning. Apart from learning new skills, they will come to understand each other better since they will know from experience what each other's domestic work involves.

In addition it is often right for an older couple to live more separately, cherishing those aspects of life which they can happily share, but giving each other the freedom to pursue divergent interests and make new friendships. It may be best to go on different holidays, and to spend the weekends engaged in different activities, according to their various tastes and interests. And it may be a great psychological relief to sleep in different bedrooms – which is likely to be possible once the children have left home. Separate bedrooms need not spell the end of sexual relations, and may even add romantic excitement; but even if the marriage does become celibate, there can still be physical affection and emotional support. Besides, as we grow older our sleeping patterns sometimes change in quite different ways; so a couple may sleep more soundly apart than together.

Divorce rates rise steeply amongst couples in late middle age; but breaking up the marriage is both unnecessary and far more damaging than people first imagine. A monk may feel he has little in common with most of his brethren, but can remain loyal to them by finding the right balance of separateness and togetherness, solitude and company. And he knows that if he destroys the trust that binds them by leaving the community, he himself will find it extremely difficult ever to trust another person. Equally divorce leaves scars of distrust which never fully heal; and marriage can almost always be preserved by adjusting this balance of being together and apart.

# TASK

Reflect on how you have altered in the past ten years, in your attitudes, values and abilities. Try and predict how you are likely to alter in the next ten years. Then ask how successful you are at adapting your pattern of life to these changes in yourself.

# HOSPITALITY

All guests should be welcomed like Christ himself . . . When they arrive and depart they should be treated with the greatest respect and courtesy . . . And special care should be shown to the poor and troubled, for their needs are Christ's needs.

Benedict

# HOSPITALITY

When St Anthony trekked out into the desert he hoped to be alone for the rest of his life. But within a few months people had sought him out to ask his advice; so if he wanted solitude he had constantly to move from cave to cave to escape his pursuers. Similarly when St Cuthbert sailed out to Farne Island and began growing his own crops, he hoped he would never see another soul. But soon there was a steady flow of people willing to risk the rough waters to speak to the saintly abbot; and he was compelled to build a special house in which they could stay. Indeed according to Bede's account the birds used to bring grease with which Cuthbert could clean his visitors' shoes, as an act of Christ-like humility. Thus hospitality is an inevitable part of monastic life, even when the monk lives as a hermit.

So when Pachomius and Benedict formed communities of monks they made provision from the outset to receive guests. And they taught that in receiving guests the monks were welcoming Christ himself, since his Spirit is present in every person. Thus they urged their monks to treat guests with respect and even reverence. But Benedict learned from bitter experience of the problems which guests can bring, and warned his monks to be on their guard. Some came simply to eat the monastery's food and sleep in its warmth, without any spiritual purpose. Others came with malicious intent, to undermine the community by spreading false rumours amongst the monks and fomenting division. Moreover the sheer quantity of guests can disturb the monks, distracting them from prayer and work both by their practical demands and by conversation. Thus since Benedict's time most monasteries have built a separate guest-house, which may be some distance from the main buildings; and they have appointed a particular monk as guest-master, with a team supporting him to cater for the guests' needs without disturbing the community as a whole. Moreover guests are not free to engage monks in conversation as they choose, but must make specific appointments through the guest-master. In this way large numbers of guests can be welcomed without threatening the monastery's integrity; and disruptive and malicious guests can do little damage.

Those of us who seek to be holy in the world do not exercise the same fascination over others as monks in caves and monasteries. Yet for all of us there are small opportunities to show hospitality. We can invite newcomers to our neighbourhood for a meal, perhaps also offering to cook food for them until they have sorted out their own cooking equipment. We can offer to look after neighbouring children while the parents go out shopping. We can indicate to those who are lonely and depressed that there is always a cup of tea and a chat in our home. And once word gets round that we are willing to have guests to stay, people will find their way to our door.

As monasteries find, we can receive great blessings from our guests: their ideas and insights can stimulate us; and their warmth and appreciation can encourage us. Yet, like monasteries, we are vulnerable. We too can find ourselves so distracted that our own daily rhythm of prayer, work and relaxation is lost. And guests staying a number of nights can be utterly exhausting, since we feel that we must be at their service from morning until evening. Moreover we can find that by constantly making ourselves available to those in distress their suffering starts to weigh us down, so eventually we also become distressed. Inevitably too we can be exploited by those whose only interest is a hot meal and a warm bed.

We must each honestly recognize our own limitations, as Benedict compelled his monks to do, and act accordingly. There is no shame in deciding not to have strangers to stay, if the burden is too great. It may be right to limit the times of the day or evening when visitors are welcome, in order to sustain the rhythm of daily life. And it is better to offer the hand of friendship to one or two people in distress, offering them solid and reliable support, than to collapse under the strain of befriending too many. Putting such boundaries around our hospitality may at times seem heartless; and, just as monasteries are sometimes criticized for keeping guests at arm's length, we may be judged harshly for refusing to extend a welcome to all people at all times. But in our hearts we know that we are being as hospitable as our energies and equanimity allow. We must merely shrug off such criticism. Besides, those who judge us are likely to be poor examples themselves – if they had an open house, they would know the difficulties.

The time of year when hospitality is most needed, and yet when we can feel most reluctant to offer it, is Christmas. In the past century we in the West have turned Christmas into a largely private affair, when families gather to eat, drink, chat – and watch television. A guest who is not already a close friend can seem like an intruder. Yet, by making Christmas so private, we have turned it into a season of acute loneliness for those who have no family to welcome or to visit. The brute fact is that the private, selfish Christmas is a blasphemy. A central facet of the Christmas story is that Mary and Joseph were refused hospitality, so the Son of God was born in a stable. Thus the true celebration of Christmas must involve opening our homes to the lonely – and thereby welcoming the Son of God into our family. Those who have celebrated Christmas in a Franciscan friary, where tramps eat turkey and plum pudding with the friars, will know that an open Christmas is far more joyful and satisfying than the closed, stuffy Christmas around the television screen.

Physically welcoming people into our homes is not, however, the only form of hospitality. Monks and nuns are usually dedicated letter-writers, maintaining a wide correspondence both with personal friends and with those who seek their advice. Sometimes a letter can be a more appropriate means of offering counsel and encouragement than a direct conversation, since the recipient of the letter has time to ponder and digest its contents over hours and days before giving a response. This can be particularly important where the advice is hard and uncomfortable: in a direct encounter the initial reaction of hurt pride and angry self-justification could preclude any proper consideration of the advice; but in the silence of reading and reflecting on a letter, the advice is more likely to be accepted. Sadly the art of letter-writing has waned in recent decades, with too many of us regarding it as a tedious and dull activity. Yet as the published correspondence of innumerable monks and other religious figures indicate, a remarkable intimacy can be achieved through the pen. Like many monks and nuns, we should consider setting aside a particular period of time each week for correspondence, so that writing letters ceases to be an unwelcome interruption of our busy schedule, and instead is part of the schedule itself.

As Benedict taught, the foundation of all hospitality should be prayer. It is through praying for those who come to see us, and for those who write, that we truly welcome them into our hearts.

## TASK

Try and list the people whom you have received into your house within the past month. Ask whether you were able to offer a warm and generous welcome. If you have enough space, aim to invite one or two people, who would otherwise be alone, to spend next Christmas with you – either for Christmas Day itself, or for the whole Christmas season.

# MISSION

Those who seek to take the Gospel to others must have both heart and mind ablaze with the fire of love.

Ignatius

# MISSION

Britain and Ireland became Christian in the fifth and sixth centuries largely through the network of monasteries that the great Celtic saints established. Patrick founded his community in Armagh, and, at the same time, Brigit set up her convent in Kildare, where they educated children, welcomed countless visitors, and nursed the sick. Within a few decades hundreds of similar communities had sprung up across Ireland taking the Gospel to the remotest regions. Columba carried the monastic vision to Scotland, where it also spread rapidly; and one of Columba's disciples, Aidan, set up a monastery on Lindisfarne, an island off the Northumbrian coast, whence the vision spread across northern England. In the meantime Iltut and David had founded communities in Wales, which also inspired innumerable imitators. The evangelization of Germany, France and, some centuries later, Russia, followed a similar pattern.

The missionary power of the monastery lay in the spiritual, emotional and material quality of its life. People could come and see that the monks lived in peace and harmony with one another, sorting out problems not by fighting, but by prayer and cooperation. This is turn enabled the monks to work extremely efficiently in clearing woodland and planting crops, so they had ample food both for their own needs and to give to the needy. The palpable success of their way of life gave the monks great confidence in themselves and their faith, so that when they went out to the neighbouring villages they could speak with clear authority about the love of Christ. Soon people had little doubt that Christianity was the route to contentment in this world, as well as bliss in the next.

By the seventh century virtually the whole of Europe was nominally Christian, so the early missionary zeal flagged. But in the twelfth century a new kind of monastic missionary emerged, the mendicant friars led by St Francis of Assisi and St Dominic. They formed small mobile communities, wandering from place to place to preach the Gospel. While the Church as a whole had grown complacent and corrupt, these holy friars sought to imitate in every particular the life of Christ and his apostles. They lived under a simple monastic rule which forbade them from owning any possessions, so that every gift they received was immediately handed on to the poor. Not surprisingly they gained huge popularity and respect amongst ordinary people, inspiring a resurgence of the Christian faith.

Today many of us feel very confused about mission. The word itself conjures up images either of heroic young men and doughty spinsters setting off for darkest Africa in the last century, or of huge rallies where charismatic preachers urge people to come forward and embrace Jesus as their personal saviour. While we may admire both types of mission, we ourselves do not feel called to live in tropical climes or to speak in public. Yet we are aware that the majority of people around us have little or no religious belief, and are indifferent to religious values. And the more closely we get to know our neighbours, the more convinced we become that a living faith could transform their discontent into joy.

While some of those early monks were great speakers, most were simple, uneducated people with no oratorical skills. And it was not words that convinced their neighbours of the truth of the Gospel, but example. Going further back in history, the main attraction of Christianity in the first two or three centuries after Christ was the quality of Christian family life. Many people in the Roman Empire regarded this strange religion from Palestine with contempt, as the crude invention of deluded peasants – just as today Christians are often looked upon with snobbish indifference. But when they saw how well Christian men treated their wives, how secure and happy were their children, and how much the Christian community supported its members in times of need, they began to take more seriously the Jewish prophet who inspired such behaviour. The visible fruits of faith gradually overcame people's intellectual doubts, so that by the time Christ-

ianity was adopted as the official religion of the empire early in
the fourth century, the majority of people had already volun-
tarily embraced it.

We are all called to this kind of mission – because we are all
called to be holy. If we are loving and faithful towards family
and friends then we are missionaries, bearing witness to the love
and faith in which we believe. Moreover if, like the Celtic monks,
our love and faith find expression in welcoming strangers, and
in visiting and caring for those who are sick or in any kind of
distress in our neighbourhood, then the power of our witness is
multiplied. We are not required to show off our good works,
or draw attention to ourselves in any way; such pride would
itself be a contradiction of our faith. People will see as much as
they need of the quality of our lives.

Monasteries have a particular evangelistic advantage, because
visitors can see the Christian faith being put into practice in
every aspect of daily life; whereas once the ordinary lay Christian leaves home for the office or factory, he must to a great
degree conform to the imperfect standards of the world. However, the local church provides a visible, open context where in
small ways our faith can be applied publicly. We should each
seek to ensure that our church is a good steward of its material
resources, conserving the environment and caring for the needy.
And we should ensure that newcomers receive a warm welcome
– not smothering them with bonhomie, but conveying simple
pleasure at their presence in our midst.

Missionaries to tropical climes and evangelistic preachers are
often judged – and judge themselves – by the numbers of converts their efforts bring. The kind of pastoral mission to which
all of us are called cannot be measured in such stark terms. If
we recall our own path to a living faith, we are aware that many
people helped to open our hearts, even though it may have been
one particular person who led us to take the final step; and most
of those people are quite unaware of the priceless service they
rendered to us. Likewise our witness of love and faith may cause
no actual conversions, but may still inspire numerous people on
their spiritual pilgrimage; and we too are likely to remain quite

ignorant of the good we do – which spares us from the temptation of pride.

# TASK

Put yourself in the position of a neighbour observing your way of life, and then ask whether your way of life seems attractive and fulfulling.

# PART 3

*Obedience*

# PRAYER

The purpose of prayer is to invite God to live inside us, so our greatest desire always is to obey his will. The mind thus becomes the temple of God, and the soul becomes his friend.

Basil

# PRAYER

Basil, the great monastic founder in the Eastern Church, taught that every moment of the monk's life should be filled with prayer. He should pray as he emerges from sleep in the morning, pray as he eats his meals, pray as he works in the fields, and even pray while he is talking with his brethren. A monk whose heart and mind are praying throughout the day will, according to Basil, find that he also prays at night, his dreams becoming images of divine love.

In order to learn to pray constantly, Basil's monks were required first to reflect deeply on the nature and purpose of prayer. Children are taught to pray by making requests of God, asking him to look after them and their families by providing for all their various needs. Thus childish prayers usually take the form of a list of wants and desires presented to God. And many adults barely move beyond this style of prayer, continuing to look to God primarily as a supernatural power who can guide events in their favour. Such prayers are not wrong. On the contrary, Basil taught making requests is the foundation of prayer, since the person praying in such a way is acknowledging his total dependence on God's love and mercy. And the mature monk should continue to set time aside each day in which to pray for particular people who are sick or in any special need. Such prayers do not, of course, change God's mind, causing him to act differently from his previous intentions. But, as Basil said, a world in which there are many people constantly putting themselves in God's hands will find itself conforming to God's laws – and thence share in his peace and joy.

Yet if requests to God are the foundation of prayer, the task of the monk, and all who wish to be monks in the world, is to erect a mighty spiritual edifice on that foundation. And, to use

Basil's metaphor, the stones of that edifice are acts of obedience. The person who prays constantly through the day is deliberately seeking to submit his own will to God's will. As he rises from his bed he offers to God the activities of the day. As he sets about his work, he asks God to guide his brain and hands, so that his decisions and actions should be divinely inspired. As he eats, he recognizes that it is God who is feeding him. And in conversation he seeks to listen to God, both to guide his own words, and to enable him to hear the true thoughts and feelings behind the other person's words.

Such a regime of constant prayer can seem quite daunting: daily life is difficult enough already without trying to remember God minute by minute. But in the seventeenth century the gentle English bishop, Thomas Ken, wrote a manual of prayer for the ordinary people of his diocese. He stipulated a series of 'ejaculations', which are simple prayers, mainly taken from the Bible, consisting of a single sentence. He urged people to learn these ejaculations by heart, and to speak them – or mutter them under their breath – at appropriate moments through the day. After a few weeks the ejaculations became virtually automatic, so they require no effort. And after a few months the words of the ejaculations melt away, and the soul prays constantly without words. Thomas Ken understood well that, compared with the monastery, the family home is noisy and chaotic, making it difficult to get into the habit of using his ejaculations. And he was aware too that some people might prefer to compose their own, or pray spontaneously in whatever phrases come into their heads. But once the habit is established – whether using written or extemporary prayers – the wife looking after her children or the husband working in the fields can pray as deeply and as continuously as the monks.

While the work of constant prayer is for each individual to perform, its effects within a monastery infuse the entire community. If each monk is submitting himself minute by minute to God, then the decisions and actions of the community will quite naturally follow God's will – and thus the monks will live in unity with one another and with their natural environment. Indeed, like the players in an orchestra, each individual monk contributes through his own prayers to a beautiful spiritual harmony. And when one monk becomes spiritually weary or depressed, the unseen prayers of the others sustain him. It is this mutual support in prayer which gives monasteries their special grace and power, so striking to the visitor. Yet to some degree, as Thomas Ken observed, this can be replicated in the world if both husband and wife strive to pray constantly, or if a group scattered within a neighbourhood come to regard themselves as a community of prayer. Indeed Ken hoped that in each parish in his diocese there would be a small number of people who would follow his manual of prayer, forming a kind of invisible monastery; and their spiritual music would inspire and uplift the whole neighbourhood.

Just as in the monastery or in a marriage there can be no pretence, since close daily contact reveals each person's true personality, so in constant prayer there can be no pretences towards God. The art of constant prayer requires that every thought and emotion, negative as well as positive, be exposed to God. At first this can feel awkward, since we quite naturally want to present only our best side to God, expressing love, gratitude and praise. But to confine our relationship with God in this way means turning away from him at times when anger, egotistical pride, jealousy and other such potentially destructive emotions rise to the surface. Yet once we pluck up courage to vent our anger at God, to unmask our proud and jealous feelings, we begin to experience the full force of his love. He does not suddenly wipe away these emotions; it was he, after all, who implanted them within the human breast. Rather he transfigures them, so that they become creative: anger is turned into a thirst for justice; egotistical pride becomes pride in our work for others; even jealousy can be turned upside down to become generosity, in which one takes pleasure in the achievements and blessings of others.

Prayer, which starts as lists of requests sent to God, gradually matures into a single, passionate desire which embraces every other want or need: the desire for union with God. There are innumerable stories of monks and nuns, such as Teresa of Avila and Catherine of Sienna, whose fervour for God overwhelmed both body and soul: their physical sexual feelings, as well as their spiritual emotions, were caught up in the conduct of prayer. And, far from detracting from practical concerns, this power of prayer enabled them to work with outstanding efficiency: Teresa founded and organized an entire order of monasteries, while Catherine ran hospitals for lepers. Few of us, perhaps, are called to such dizzy spiritual heights, or to such noble acts of charity. Yet as the years pass so the practice of constant prayer gradually narrows the gulf between earth and heaven, so that even washing the dishes or mending a fuse become an offering of love towards God.

## TASK

Write out a series of six or seven 'ejaculations' which you might utter through the course of a typical day. Then learn them by heart, and try using them.

# WORSHIP

The glory of God is revealed in a living person. And the true life of all people consists in glorifying God.

Clare

# WORSHIP

Benedict described the corporate worship of the monastery as the work of God; and he saw worship as the primary function of the monk. So just as the carpenter spends eight hours each day cutting wood and making furniture, as the farmer spends eight hours sowing and reaping, the monk spends a similar time singing God's praises. Indeed for the past fifteen centuries Western monasteries have had a least four services, and in some cases as many as eight services, in each twenty-four hour period – including very often a service in the middle of the night. And at the heart of their worship is usually a daily celebration of the Eucharist.

Any lay person who attends a monastic service is awe-struck by its beauty. Monks, who individually may be musically untal-ented, learn through constant repetition to sing the psalms and canticles in precise harmony; and even the prayers are spoken together in perfect unison, in which the rhythms and cadences of the phrases are perfectly captured. Yet to many lay people the purpose of this time-consuming work is unclear. Those who attend services only on Sunday typically regard worship as a means of restoring their spiritual and moral balance, so that they can function better in their daily lives; it is a means to an end. And if this can be achieved by spending only an hour or two in church on Sunday morning they see no point in attending additional services. Not surprisingly growing numbers in the past century or more have concluded that there are other, more congenial methods of spiritual refreshment, such as going for a walk in the countryside or local park, or sitting at home in the comfort of an armchair listening to music – such as a recording of monastic plainchant. The worship of the monastery is, to the modern mind, akin to the opera or painting or sculpture: it is beautiful, and even inspiring, for those who participate in it, or who appreciate it; but it is totally useless.

To the monk, however, worship is not a means to an end, but an end in itself. It is his primary pleasure, as well as his work. And, if asked to explain its meaning, he will compare the services in church with heaven itself. In heaven we will be gathered together in God's presence, enjoying his love without any ulterior purpose; likewise in worship we deliberately come together to acknowledge God in our midst, and to rejoice in his grace. And, just as in heaven we will no longer need to strive and struggle, but simply rest in God's peace, so also in corporate worship we are each carried by the ancient words and music, our unruly thoughts and feelings directed towards God. Moreover the services which punctuate the day give outward expression to the constant private prayer which should accompany our every activity, so that even the most mundane chores become a spiritual preparation for praising God in church. Thus, rather than worship being a spiritual tool to help us in our daily lie, it is the goal to which our life on earth should be aimed.

Benedict wrote of how the pots and pans in the kitchen should be treated with the same reverence as the vessels on the altar with which the Eucharist is celebrated. To him the Eucharist symbolized the entire life and purpose of the monastery, and so should be in the centre of its worship. The bread and wine are signs of the monks' labour; thus in offering bread and wine on the altar, this labour is made holy. By consuming from the same loaf and the same cup, the monks are symbolically unified in God's love. And, since the Eucharist is a holy meal in which all share equally, the monks express their commitment to justice and equity in all things. In the last century the great Christian socialist, F. D. Maurice, urged people to carry Benedict's eucharistic teaching out of the monasteries into the grimy industrial cities of Europe, so that production and consumption in the modern economy could also be made holy. And happily in recent decades Christians from every tradition have come to see the centrality of the Eucharist as the supreme symbol of a godly life.

Yet even if we adopt the monastic attitude to worship, few of us in the world could match four services each day, or even a daily Eucharist. Indeed the pressures of work and family make it difficult to get to a church at all during the week. Thomas Cranmer, who compiled the Book of Common Prayer in the sixteenth century, tried to solve this dilemma by condensing the monastic pattern of worship into two services, Morning and Evening Prayer, that could be used by families at home. And numerous devout families gathered twice each day, before breakfast and again before supper, to say Cranmer's services – the most famous of such families being the Ferrars at Little Gidding, who were actually accused by some rabid anti-Catholics of running a 'nunnery'. Other families found two acts of worship too demanding, and so used only one of Cranmer's services. In this they were unconsciously imitating the Coptic monastic pattern in which the monks are more free and less communal than in the Benedictine community: they worship together only once, usually in the early morning, allowing each to develop his own form of private prayer through the rest of the day.

Whatever pattern of worship is adopted, the key is strict regularity. A husband and wife, or a group of friends, must stipulate a particular time when they meet for worship, whether at home or in a church – and stick to it. At first this may seem quite oppressive, and we may even find ourselves feeling angry at such a restriction on our liberty. But soon coming together for worship at the same moment every day becomes a habit, like cleaning one's teeth or making one's bed, that one performs without a thought. For most people the early morning is the best time, before the telephone is liable to ring or the rush of the day begins – and when mind and spirit are fresh. But for others the late evening may be spiritually preferable and more convenient. It is probably a mistake to try and fix a time during the main part of the day, because for most of us the timetable of activities is too variable. It is important, especially when worshipping in the morning, to stipulate a time by which the service must end, restraining the occasional desire to present God with too long a list of requests or to be too effusive in his praise. There is nothing more distracting than anxiety about the clock – and people can only relax into their worship if they are sure that later commitments in the day will not be broken.

Over the centuries there have been few disputes in the Church more fierce than those over forms and styles of worship. Far from seeing style as a matter of personal taste and culture, people have imagined themselves to be fighting over matters of high theological principle. If worship is conducted daily, the only matter of importance is that it should be of a form which can be sustained, month by month and year by year. Thus, as monasteries have found, it should be simple, even austere, since complex ritual soon grows stale; but, as the monastic office exemplifies, simplicity does not preclude great beauty. Again, learning from the monasteries, a period of silent meditation is very valuable, since meditation conducted in a group is often far deeper and more creative than one's attempts at meditation alone. And extemporary prayers for the sick and the needs of the world should avoid undue verbosity or repetitive religious formulae: a few words to focus people's minds on a particular person or problem is sufficient. As for leading worship, the form should be so straightforward that anyone can conduct the service; so husband and wife, or members of the group, can take it in turns. If even a tone-deaf monk can learn to chant lauds and vespers, any of us can learn to lead a simple act of worship.

## TASK

Find a simple form of daily worship, such as that contained in the Taizé Offices or the Little Gidding Prayer Book. Then for a trial period of a week or a month, set a time each day when you use this form of worship, either on your own, or preferably with your spouse or a friend.

# BELIEF

Understanding is the reward, not the cause of faith. Therefore seek not to understand that you may believe, but believe that you may understand.

Augustine

# BELIEF

In the 1960s the American monk Thomas Merton began to make close contacts with monks and teachers of other faiths, and eventually travelled to Asia to talk and pray with Hindus, Buddhists and Muslims. He himself remained a devout and unshakeable Roman Catholic, steeped in the doctrine and liturgy of his Church. But as he grew closer to monks from the Oriental traditions, he discovered that their spiritual experiences were akin to his own. Holiness, he realized, is not confined to Christianity, but is the aspiration of religions across the globe.

Merton was treading a path of unity that many have walked before. As long ago as the fourteenth century Mother Julian could not bring herself to believe the orthodox doctrine that people of other faiths are eternally damned. She can only have known about Islam and Oriental religions from rather garbled and embellished travellers' tales. But she had gleaned enough to conclude that they could be as devout in their worship of God and as charitable towards their neighbours as Christians. Even earlier another follower of the monastic way, Francis of Assisi, travelled to Palestine in the midst of the Crusades to try and make peace between Christianity and Islam; he is said both to have impressed the Islamic leaders, and been impressed by them. More recently, as communications between East and West have improved, there has developed a vigorous spiritual trade between monks of all faiths, with various forms of yoga being practised in many Christian monasteries, while Christian mystical works are eagerly read in many Hindu ashrams. Those who aspire to holiness, it seems, are happy and willing to gain wisdom from elsewhere.

Sadly this hidden monastic tolerance is not emulated in the public affairs of religions or nations. People of every faith believe that their doctrinal formulae encapsulate the truth, so that other formulae are either inadequate or wrong. And they fondly imagine that God uniquely blesses their endeavours. As those who are opposed to religion frequently observe, history is littered with religious wars, in which one sect seeks to dominate the rest. And today countries remain divided, and people are oppressed and tortured on religious grounds. Religious conflicts are, of course, often closely interwoven with politics, with kings and dictators exploiting religious fervour for their cause. But this does not excuse religious leaders from allowing themselves to be exploited.

To Thomas Merton religious doctrines were not precise expressions of divine truth, but windows through which the truth might be discerned. And, like glass, doctrines are fashioned by humans, their clarity and transparency as spiritual windows depending on the skill and insight of their theological craftsmen. Merton himself had discovered the glories of Roman Catholic doctrine as a young man, after some years of restless debauchery; and he never ceased to marvel at the truth he had learned through Catholic theology, encouraging others to share his experience. Moreover he recognized that there are many evil religious doctrines, promulgated by corrupt or misguided teachers, through which falsehood is seen masquerading as truth. But when it comes to the great religions of the world, he had no doubt that their doctrines are windows on divine truth. And the doctrinal differences between religions, which to the logical mind might suggest contradictions, are due to the different angles and shapes of the windows, and the different distortions in the glass. The proof of this spiritual unity lies in the lives of the people who live wholeheartedly by those doctrines: the holiness of the Hindu or Buddhist monk is identical to that of the Christian monk.

Like Thomas Merton, we who are Christians should be strong and fervent in the basic doctrines of our faith. The belief that God's Word was made flesh in Jesus Christ, and thence Jesus Christ was perfect man, assures us that we too can aspire to perfection – to be perfectly holy, as he was. The knowledge of his suffering and death assures us that he fully understands the very worst suffering and temptation that we may face – thus he can strengthen and encourage us in the way of holiness. And faith in his resurrection holds out the promise of perfect and eternal joy at the end of that way – joy which we can taste with increasing frequency as the journey progresses. Yet these, or any other formulations, of our basic doctrines are grotesquely imperfect expressions of the Christian Gospel, since the sublime truth of the Gospel is beyond words. So if we assert that such formulations embody divine truth, and thus turn the doctrines themselves into objects of faith, we are in fact worshipping idols – idols constructed not of wood or stone, but of words. Worse still, we soon use these idols as verbal sticks with which to beat those who do not accept them. Thus most religious conflicts centre on disputes about doctrines, rather than on any disagreement about ultimate truth.

In a world divided by religion – and by religion mixed with politics – those who feel called to tread the path of holiness can show the way to unity. That path cuts through the artificial barriers of creeds, so that people of every faith can join the journey. As Christians of a particular denomination, our first act of unity is to pray and worship with other denominations. This does not mean striving for some common forms of worship which all can accept, nor trying to join together the different ecclesiastical organizations; rather, the purpose is to make spiritual bonds, and thence become friends and partners in the spiritual pilgrimage. Beyond Christian ecumenism comes the unity of different religions. Here too there is no substitute for personal contact, visiting temples, synagogues and mosques to pray with Hindus, Buddhists, Jews and Muslims. And if in advance of such contacts we have read their scriptures and holy books, so we have already drunk from their spiritual waters, and warm friendships will be quickly made. Indeed the greatest compliment we can pay to another faith is to enjoy its spiritual traditions.

In the opening verses of his gospel, St John wrote of the Word as the agent of creation, 'through whom all things were made'. The Word 'became flesh' in the person of Jesus Christ, so Christians in their relationship with Jesus are in direct contact with the Word, and thence with God. Yet since the Word is also manifest in all creation, we should expect to find divine truth made manifest in every religion, in every human being, and in every animal and plant. It is the desire to discern God's Word in every aspect of his created order which lies at the root of true, divinely-inspired belief.

## TASK

Write out your own creed, putting down all the basic religious and moral beliefs to which you subscribe. Be absolutely honest, avoiding any statement that you feel you ought to accept, but cannot in truth believe.

# STUDY

The purpose of study is to help the soul of the person who studies, and thereby enable him to help the souls of others.

Ignatius

# STUDY

Although some religious orders, such as the Jesuits, are renowned for the sharp minds of their monks, recruiting almost exclusively people of academic ability, most monasteries contain the whole range of intellectual capacities. A typical Benedictine community may contain a handful of theologians and philosophers, able to pen learned papers on abstruse matters of doctrine, plus a much larger number able to learn enough theology and philosophy to pass exams in the subjects. In addition there will be people whose mental talents are more practical, enabling them to repair the monastery vehicles and maintain the buildings. And there may be monks whose education was a failure, leaving them unable even to compose a letter. Yet every monk, regardless of ability and inclination, is required to devote some time each day to study, reading and digesting books that will deepen his faith. And at mealtimes a monk reads out loud a book that will feed his brethren's minds and souls, while they feed their bodies.

The reason for this emphasis on study is that the intellect is one of the faculties which God has bestowed upon us in order to perceive and know him. Prayer and worship, to which most monks devote far longer hours, appeal mainly to the imagination and intuition, as well as to the emotions. Thus the monk's devotions must be completed by reading works that will deepen his mental understanding of God's love.

The range of books which monks read can be seen by a visit to a monastery library. It includes works of theology as well as biblical studies. But its central area is spirituality: works written by men and women of profound holiness, reflecting on their spiritual pilgrimage. Indeed many of the great mystical works, such as *The Cloud of Unknowing* and *The Imitation of Christ*, were probably written for monks and nuns. In addition there is a strong emphasis on ecclesiastical and social history, so that monks and nuns can see how their own way of life is rooted within a long and venerable tradition. And for light relief biography and the classic novels are encouraged.

In past centuries most ordinary men and women could only envy the literary interests of the monk and nun: few people could read, and even those who did possess a rudimentary education could not afford books. But since the late nineteenth century, as literacy and wage rates began to rise steeply throughout the Western world, so large numbers have come to regard spiritual reading as an essential part of their religious devotion. Most of the mystical classics have been translated and published in popular editions, and now adorn innumerable bookshelves – and, more importantly, nestle with the alarm clock and the spectacle case on bedside tables. Many theologians and biblical scholars have taken the trouble to produce short and accessible accounts of the main issues in their fields, as well as providing notes and commentaries on the Bible itself to aid people in their scriptural studies. And there are many good modern works on spirituality, some written by monks and nuns, which present ancient wisdom in modern dress.

But many of us, as we wander round a bookshop, can feel quite confused, and even frightened, not knowing which books best meet our present needs, nor what subjects we should study. And, besides, the sheer volume of material available can overwhelm us. From the earliest centuries of monasticism each monk had a spiritual director – sometimes known as a 'soul friend' – who not only heard his confession, but also directed his studies. Thus the spiritual director would give the monk a book, asking him perhaps to note down his own thoughts and reactions as he read it; then at their next meeting they would discuss the book – and in the light of their discussion the spiritual director would suggest further reading. Thus the monk in effect followed a course of study tailored to suit his particular requirements.

Such spiritual directors are rare in the world. But there are different ways of receiving the same guidance. Some of us like to pursue a formal course, in which the syllabus and the reading list has been set in advance. And now there are a number of institutes and colleges which put on such courses, which can be done either by correspondence or through seminars and lectures. The drawback, however, is that the individual must stick rigidly to the prescribed path, even if his own heart and mind are yearning to go off at a tangent. Alternatively a group of friends living near each other can meet together every week, fortnight or month, for shared study. They can decide between themselves what books to read and discuss; and when they are uncertain, they can seek outside advice. Although the method lacks the expert guidance which a formal course can provide, it can be far more flexible and responsive to personal needs.

If a monk can sometimes listen to a Jane Austen novel or a biography of Napoleon while eating his dinner, then we too should be quite broad in our spiritual study. Undoubtedly good fiction offers the most profound insights into the human soul, and biography can inspire us with moral goodness or appal us with evil in equal measure. Above all, poetry can penetrate the divine mystery itself: in this century the finest mysticism is to be found in the verses of that monastic poet, Gerard Manley Hopkins. Some monasteries now play recorded music at the evening meal, knowing that Bach and Beethoven not only relax the mind but also uplift the soul. And with careful selection one can find television and radio programmes of which even Benedict and Pachomius would have approved.

The greatest problem, however, is time. In the monastery, where every moment of the day is ordered, the monk finds himself with an hour allocated to study; and, while he may occasionally nod off with a book in his hand, he has no choice but to try and improve his mind in that period. In the world, by contrast, finding even half an hour during the day when the telephone does not ring, the children do not scream, or there is not some urgent demand to be met, is for most of us well-nigh impossible. Besides, it is extremely hard to wrench one's mind from the whirl of worldly concerns onto a mystical treatise. We face, of course, precisely the same difficulty in getting down to private prayer and meditation. And the solution is identical. We must make time in the early morning or the late evening –

depending on when the mind and heart are most receptive –
when we both study and pray. And we must stick to that time
like a limpet to a rock.

## TASK

Reflect on whether you are finding it easy or difficult to allocate time to study this book. Ask whether there are ways of making study easier, perhaps by allocating a particular time of day to it. Think of two or three books you could study after finishing this one.

# CONFESSION

People sometimes ask what monks do in a monastery. The answer is that we fall and get up, we fall and get up, and fall and get up again. And we find the strength to get up by confessing our weakness to God.

Pachomius

# CONFESSION

Monks are not special or peculiar people. God seems to choose at random those whom he wants to enter a monastery. So in every monastic community one will find people of every type of temperament and personality. There are plump, phlegmatic monks, who smile and laugh easily, and who remain calm amidst chaos. There are wiry, choleric monks, whose thoughts are profound and emotions fiery. There are languid, melancholic monks, whose imaginative fantasies distract their minds from the humdrum world of cold cells and hot kitchens. And there are bustling, sanguine monks, who are always optimistic and keen to get on with the job at hand. Indeed a monastery boasts the same mixture of characters as any village or town.

But monks do have one trait in common, which many of the rest of us do not share: they acknowledge their own guilt. They feel impelled towards the monastic life because they know their lives are not right, and thus they need help and guidance. Thus they are very willing to be members of, in Benedict's phrase, a 'school for sinners'. Many imagine that as soon as they enter the monastery and participate in its worship and activities their guilt will melt away. They soon find, however, that the holiness of the monastic life seems to make this burden even heavier, since they feel themselves so inadequate as servants of God. Then they discover that at the very heart of the monastic life lies the ancient practice of confession, through which they can face God directly – and allow him to lift off this burden of guilt from their shoulders. And once confession has become a regular part of their spiritual discipline, so that the weight of guilt is no longer holding them down, they will be able gradually to rise up the 'ladder of perfection'.

We are all similarly burdened with guilt, the difference being that many of us refuse to admit this fact. Indeed the main reason why we fight shy of the holy life is that we cannot bear to look at the burden of guilt which need to be lifted. Moreover in the course of this century popular psychology has taught us to regard guilt itself as intrinsically unhealthy; so to acknowledge the presence of guilt in our hearts is to see ourselves as psychologically disordered.

To free ourselves from guilt, we must begin by accepting that guilt is a perfectly natural and even essential human emotion. A child learns how to behave because he is eager for his parents' approval and fearful of their disapproval; by the tone of their voices parents can guide their children, gradually instilling a sense of guilt which prevents them doing wrong – and encourages them to act rightly. Thus the propensity for guilt is innate, and the role of the parents is to nurture children's guilt so that it will function well in adult life. Without guilt children could only be taught moral values by sticks and carrots, punishments and rewards – as animals are trained.

The problem, to which more enlightened psychology often points, is that our sense of guilt is often misinformed and distorted, since parents pass on to their children their own moral and emotional confusions. Thus, for example, many people in the West still feel profound guilt about sex, regarding all sexual feeling and activity as dirty. Almost as common is a strange guilt about excelling at any sport or task, as if doing better than others was in itself selfish and insulting. Indeed any of us could discover within ourselves a range of matters, some utterly trivial, which can induce a quite misguided guilty response. Moreover, even when our sense of guilt is appropriately directed, it can often not be assuaged merely by avoiding actions which evoke guilt. A feeling of personal and moral inadequacy – of not being worthy of either the approval or the love of others – hangs like a shadow over our lives.

We try to escape this shadow in all manner of ways. Some of us exhaust ourselves by good works, rushing from one charitable activity to another, as if the sheer quantity of such benevolence would alleviate guilt. Others adopt extreme political positions, partly because politics offers a way of avoiding spiritual problems, and partly because political revolution seems to offer a clear, bright future in which moral doubt and confusion have been eradicated. Most commonly, however, we are quite disproportionately frightened of any kind of criticism, avoiding situations that might make us vulnerable to adverse comment, and displaying acute offence when such comments are made. But, of course, none of these strategies work. When we perform acts of charity out of a sense of personal inadequacy, we are constantly looking for gratitude and admiration; and when this fails to be given, we are left feeling sullen and resentful. Extreme politics can offer fragile satisfaction so long as there is no opportunity to put the ideas into practice, which would shatter the utopian illusion; yet eventually the futility of such politics itself destroys the illusion. And fear of criticism merely avoids the problem of personal inadequacy, without solving it.

Confession in the wider Church is often a rather formal, perfunctory affair. It may simply entail a general confession of sin in the middle of a service, in which everyone utters the same words. And even if it involves the individual speaking to a priest, there is a formula which can readily be followed. But in many monasteries confession can be a lengthy and profound affair, in which the innermost secrets of the monk's heart are explored. In the Coptic monasteries of Egypt and Ethiopia the monk and his confessor – who is usually an older member of the community – sit facing one another in the confessor's cell, and conduct a conversation in which the confessor may ask the most penetrating questions. In this way, over the months and years, the true sources of guilt are laid bare. The confessor is not, however, acting in his own power; he is representing God. Thus at the end of the session he asks the monk to draw together all he has said in a prayer to God. He then pronounces absolution, both assuring the monk of God's forgiveness for past sins, and urging the monk to obey more closely God's moral law in the future.

Today this ancient monastic practice is beginning to be adopted more widely, not only by members of churches, but also by those with no religious affiliation. Growing numbers are recognizing that guilt is not some cancerous mental growth from which a minority of disturbed people suffer, but is a universal human trait. And far from trying to cure it by cutting it out, we must ensure that it operates in a healthy and creative manner. Thus they seek out someone with whom they can explore their own innermost feelings, and in particular discover the source of their own sense of guilt and inadequacy. Then they have a double task: firstly to recognize that the feelings of guilt which undermine self-confidence are misplaced, and thence to redirect those feelings; and secondly to learn ways of living more closely in accordance with those feelings of guilt which give healthy, appropriate signals. This process is now often known as 'counselling' rather than 'confession', but in essence it is the same: the reassurance which the confessor gives is equivalent to the pronouncement of God's forgiveness; and the working out of better ways of living accords with the confessor's moral injunctions.

If a monk in a monastery, with all the moral support and protection that a monastic community provides, needs a confessor, then we in the world are in even greater need of spiritual and moral counsel. For some of us it may be possible to have a confessor in the traditional way. Others may prefer the more modern style of counsellor. But, as Aelred of Rievaulx taught, the same needs can be fulfilled by a good, honest friend who is able to listen closely to our thoughts and feelings, and offer strong, unvarnished advice. Indeed a friend is more able to give reassurance, because he is giving counsel out of love, rather than as a professional task. But whether we have confessor, counsellor or friend, the spiritual work which they must help us to perform is vital for our mental and moral health.

## TASK

Jot down all the things which you do, or fail to do, which make
you feel guilty. Then mark those where guilt seems appropriate,
and cross out those where guilt is misdirected.

# EQUANIMITY

We believe that God is present everywhere, and that he is watching over all that we do. Thus at every moment we must be sure that we are doing his work. In this way we shall find inward peace.

Benedict

# EQUANIMITY

Visitors to monasteries are often struck by the calm and tranquillity, both of the place itself and of its inhabitants. The monks appear to live in harmony and amity, and their prayerful love seems to impregnate the walls of the buildings, so a spirit of peace rests over the community. But conversations with the monks themselves reveal a rather different story. They may relate violent scenes in the kitchen when one monk empties a saucepan of pasta over another; they may describe bitter jealousy over the allocation of cells, with monks stamping their feet and cursing the abbot because they have been given poky rooms overlooking the dustbins; and they will undoubtedly tell of times when a spirit of anger seems to blow like a hot, dry wind through the cloisters and corridors of the monastery. A community which to the outsider is serene may to the insider be tense and troubled.

There is a single explanation of this paradox. The spiritual and emotional struggle within the monastery is disciplined: through prayer, and through an unending cycle of confession and forgiveness, the monks are striving to direct all their emotions towards God. Even the spectacular failures of love – the saucepan of pasta over a monk's head – are caught within the net of prayer. As Thomas Merton has taught, holiness does not consist in suppressing or ignoring anger and aggression, since these are natural elements in the human psyche. Rather it consists in harnessing them as sources of mental and physical vigour – and insofar as we succeed in this, our life is peaceful and harmonious. The monks themselves are often acutely aware of the times when the harness breaks, and violent emotions run wild. But at most times an atmosphere of hard-working, energetic tranquillity pervades the monastery, as the monks succeed in channelling their aggressive emotions toward creative purposes – and it is this atmosphere which the visitor senses.

In addition to prayer and confession, the monks have two further allies in achieving equanimity. Firstly the steady rhythm of daily life in the monastery, while very taxing and demanding, gives little stimulus to the aggressive emotions. Indeed one of the most striking aspects of monastic life is the extraordinary amount of work they do, with so little stress – and this is entirely due to their firm, unchanging routine. Secondly, such stress as they do suffer can be dissipated in manual labour. In almost every monastic rule the monks are required to spend up to four or six hours each day wielding a spade or pushing a mop. And it is far better to take out violent anger on a clod of earth or a stubborn mark on the floor than on a fellow monk.

Today in western society stress is a major cause of unhappiness, ill health and premature death. A manager in an office may in a typical day find himself in a score of situations which evoke an aggressive response: a sale needs to be clinched with a customer, beating a rival firm; an awkward junior manager complains unreasonably about his working conditions; a young trainee arrives late for work for the third time in a week; the managing director demands an explanation for the month's poor production figures – and so on. Worse still, on his way to and from the office he may have to drive through thick traffic, or stand on a crowded train. And, as the tension builds up in his body and mind, he has no means of releasing it through physical activity. So by the time he arrives home he may take two or three hours to unwind and relax.

Far from avoiding stressful situations, many of us soon find ourselves seeking them out. Indeed at the weekends, instead of quietly digging the garden or going for a walk, we drive long distances along crowded roads to pleasure parks and seaside resorts, where our aggressive emotions receive further stimulus. The reason is that stress is addictive: the body and mind become dependent on the stress reaction, in which the heart beats faster, the muscles grow taut and the senses are heightened – just as we can become hooked on drugs. As a consequence for many people the prospect of a day of real leisure or of quiet manual activity is quite frightening: like the drug addict deprived of his shot in the arm, they would suffer painful symptoms of withdrawal.

And in the long run the effects of continued stress can be just as devastating as those of drugs. At first there are minor – although distressing – disorders, such as insomnia, facial twitching and severe headaches. But as the years pass, so the likelihood of severe diseases rises sharply: heart disease, hypertension, diabetes, cancers, and also mental illnesses such as manic depression. Without doubt excessive stress reduces both the quantity and the quality of life.

If prayer is the foundation of monastic equanimity, then prayer is the best start in curing stress. Spending ten or fifteen minutes in silence each day, aided perhaps by a reading from scripture, is itself an antidote to stress. But, more particularly, through prayer we can put ourselves in God's hands, asking him to guide us towards equanimity – and to give us the courage to accept his guidance. Our lives are so varied that the guidance will differ greatly from one person to another. A busy manager may need to work shorter hours, go swimming each morning before arriving at the office, and refuse to answer the telephone between certain hours – or he may have to resign his present job, and seek work more suited to his temperament. A young mother driven to distraction by her small children may need to exercise firmer discipline on her offspring, and be stricter with herself in accomplishing the household chores – and she may have to consider employing others to look after her children for a few hours each day, while she undertakes a paid job. But in every case equanimity can only be enjoyed when there is a constant and steady rhythm in the activities of the day, and when that rhythm includes some physical exercise.

Just as aggression itself is natural, so also is a firm daily routine. Our distant ancestors in the forest had to go out every morning, without fail, to collect berries and seeds and to kill animals for their dinner. And while the climax of the hunt was usually stressful, requiring every ounce of aggression to be successful, the stress was healthily absorbed through running and throwing spears. In the afternoon they had to grind the seeds and skin the animals, as well as sharpen their spears for tomorrow's hunt. In its own peculiar way, monastic life is an imitation of life in the forest; and so monks have long been famous for their glowing good health, their mental balance, and their longevity. If we too, in our peculiar way, can imitate our primitive ancestors, we will enjoy the same benefits. This may mean earning less money in a less stressful job – but that is a small price to pay for a peaceful mind.

## TASK

Recalling the past seven days, make a diary of how you spent your time. Then look at the diary, asking whether you are using your time in ways that are both fulfilling and sustainable, or whether you are suffering undue stress which will eventually damage your health.

# SLEEP

As we compose ourselves in mind and body for sleep, we should think of ourselves as releasing the mind and body into the loving arms of God.

Teresa

# SLEEP

Benedict allowed his monks only five hours in bed during the summer months; and even this short period was interrupted by night prayers in the chapel, so the monks slept for three hours in the early part of the night, and a further two hours later. In the winter the rule was relaxed to allow them a full nine hours in bed. But the purpose was not to have more sleep; rather, they remained in bed to keep warm, and were expected to spend the extra hours in silent meditation. Benedict's rule, severe as it was, marked in many people's eyes a decline from the rigours of the first monks in the desert. Men like Anthony and Pachomius regarded all sleep as an indulgence, believing that the devout monk should subsist on as little sleep as his mind and body would allow.

This monastic attitude to sleep remained prevalent for over a thousand years, as did their attitude to food. So the devout Christian throughout the medieval period ate sparingly and slept little. But by the eighteenth and nineteenth centuries the popular view had gone to the other extreme. The man whose body was shrouded in a thick layer of fat, and who slept for eight or more hours each night, was regarded as fit and healthy. Indeed people complimented each other on their plumpness, and inquired each morning of one another whether they had had a good night's sleep – by which they meant a long night of sleep. Today we have returned to the monastic attitude to food, at least in relation to the amount we eat, and yet retain a Victorian attitude to sleep. The healthy person now is supposed to be slim, with no surplus fat, but be able to slumber for at least a third of their lives.

Philosophers, and more recently scientists, have speculated about the meaning and process of sleep, without penetrating its mysteries. We do not know precisely what causes us to fall asleep, nor what purpose sleep serves. Amongst animals who hibernate one function of sleep is to conserve energy during the barren winter months; and perhaps we pass the nights in slumber because in the forest, where we evolved, hunting and gathering food was impossible in darkness. Sleep also rests the brain and the body – although, as scientists have shown, we can relax quite adequately while still awake. But on one thing ancient monks and modern researchers are agreed: that we can survive and flourish on much less sleep than most people take or think they need. Recent experiments have demonstrated the wisdom of Benedict's rule, that five hours of slumber is quite sufficient. If we gradually reduce our time in bed the pattern of sleep adapts, so that we actually enjoy more deep sleep, while almost entirely eliminating light sleep – thus we actually feel more refreshed on less sleep.

Insomnia is one of the most common ailments for which people visit the doctor; and huge quantities of sleeping pills are prescribed, despite their drastic side effects of which we are now aware – and despite too the fact that their beneficial effects wear off after a few weeks. Some people complain that they cannot easily fall asleep, while others are anxious because they awake early. There are various causes of insomnia, and all can be overcome by emulating monastic discipline. The first is that you are trying to sleep for longer hours than the body either wants or needs. Thus, rather than be worried about getting too little sleep, it is better like the desert monks to rejoice at the greater opportunity this gives for prayer and meditation – or unlike the monks enjoy spending more time reading and watching television. This cause of apparent insomnia is especially prevalent amongst the elderly who tend to be unable to stay asleep for long periods, but equally cannot remain awake for so long. The elderly are the major users of sleeping drugs in order to obtain 'a good night's sleep'. Under Benedict's regime the older monks were allowed to take one or two naps in the course of the day. This is the solution for all older people who can only manage three, four or five hours sleep at night, and yet feel sleepy during the day: do not struggle to extend the night's sleep, but take a nap after lunch, and another one in the early evening. And many younger people can find a short nap at midday rejuvenates them for the afternoon.

The second common cause of insomnia is irregularity of hours. Falling asleep, unlike eating, is not something which we do as an act of will; rather it is something which happens to us involuntarily. And the process of sleeping and waking is controlled by the body clock within the brain. It can take two or three days for this body clock to shift by a single hour, and up to a fortnight for it to shift by eight hours – as people whose work involves changing shifts, and who frequently travel the world into different time zones, can testify. Monasteries maintain a rigid routine, retiring and rising at exactly the same time every day; thus the body clock becomes perfectly synchronized with this routine, enabling the monks to fall asleep and waken at the right times. Many of us in the world sleep badly because we are constantly changing our pattern, staying up late for a party on some nights, and lying in bed until mid-morning at the weekends. Rising at the same hour every morning, and trying to get to bed at the same time at night, soon brings sound slumber.

The third cause is the food and drink we consume. It is widely known that tea and coffee are stimulants, causing the heart to beat faster, the muscles to grow tense, and the brain to become alert. Yet many people who complain of poor sleep continue to drink tea and coffee late in the evening. Tobacco – or, more precisely, nicotine – is also a stimulant, so smoking can cause insomnia. The counsel of perfection is to give up all stimulants at all times – which would also include chocolate, cola drinks and some other carbonated drinks that have been laced with caffeine. And some stricter monasteries follow this rule, on the grounds that stimulants and depressants are harmful to the soul as well as the body. But if such a high standard is impossible, they should obviously be avoided in the evening. Alcohol, which is a depressant, may help to induce sleep, but drunken sleep is fitful and unrefreshing, and also tends to be short. So, as Benedict prescribes for his monks, we should confine our drinking to moderate quantities in the evening.

Ethiopian monks have for many years taught that excessive

food prevents the body and mind from relaxing, and thus inhibits prayer and meditation – and sleep. As recent research has demonstrated, the body's metabolic rate adjusts upwards and downwards according to the amount we eat, especially of carbohydrates. Thus those who eat very sparingly tend to have a very low metabolic rate – which may in turn enable them to sleep more easily and soundly.

The fourth cause is stress. Persistently high levels of nervous stress can induce a whole range of illnesses, including ultimately heart disease; and it also lowers our resistance to viruses and infections. In some cases it does not interfere with sleep, but for many people stress soon leads to insomnia. In the short run this can trap the sufferer into a most distressing vicious circle: as the sufferer feels increasingly tired during the day, he finds himself becoming even more stressed as he struggles to remain alert – which in turn worsens the insomnia at night. But in the long run insomnia is nature's way of forcing the mind and body to slow down, since a point is reached where it is impossible to fight the fatigue – a point which is commonly described as a 'breakdown'. It is, of course, far better to heed the warning before the breakdown is reached.

The greatest mystery of sleep is dreaming. In every religion there are stories of how dreams accurately predicted future events. But as both religion and psychology have taught, dreams are most valuable in offering insight into our own deepest feelings and emotions: in dreams attitudes, which in our waking state we cannot admit, find expression. Thus dreams, when remembered, can provide grist for prayer and meditation. Indeed in Ethiopia, where dreams have always played a central part in religious experience, those seeking holiness are urged to pray as they fall asleep and pray as they awake, so praying and dreaming merge. And if sleep initially refuses to come, prayer is far more effective than any drug in inducing sound slumber.

## TASK

Recalling the past seven days, make a diary of when you fell asleep and woke up, and also when you felt sleepy during the day. Then assess whether you are sleeping well and efficiently, or whether a different pattern may be better.

# HOLIDAYS

During our holy-days we do not simply remember events from the past, such as the birth of Jesus and his resurrection. These events happen again within our hearts, and we become part of them.

Philip Neri

# HOLIDAYS

In the strict Coptic monasteries of Ethiopia the monks eat only cold beans and bread from Monday to Saturday. So when they gather for dinner on Sunday, they take great pleasure in eating a piping hot stew made from meat and vegetables. During Advent and Lent the regime is even stricter, with bread only during the week and hot beans on Sunday. Thus when during the twelve days between Christmas and Epiphany, and during the eight days of the Easter Octave, they have a meat and vegetable stew at every dinner, they are overjoyed. The celebration of the Sabbath and of the major festivals is reflected too in their worship. During the week, and during Advent and Lent, they sing no hymns and wear their drab, grey habits. But on Sunday they sing hymns and dress in colourful robes; and at festivals they dance and wave brightly-coloured sticks as well.

The Ethiopian monks also go on pilgrimage to restore their spirits. They recognize that if a monk stays within the monastery throughout the year, he may become torpid and listless, unable to enjoy either his worship or his work. Moreover he loses a sense of moral perspective, becoming upset at small mishaps within the monastery, and expressing severe anger over quite trivial issues. So a monk can choose to go away for a few weeks or even months, to visit another monastery or a church of some special importance. Some monks prefer to go alone, but others go in groups, inviting local lay people to join them, so that lively conversation can lighten the tedium of the journey – as it did in Chaucer's account of the Canterbury pilgrims. When a monk returns from such a trip, his zest for monastic life is usually revived, and his sense of humour at the petty tribulations of the monastery restored.

In northern Europe the Protestant reformers of the sixteenth century were extremely suspicious of pilgrimages, and in some places banned them. They rightly feared that the places to which people travelled – or, more precisely, the sacred objects within those places, such as the relics of a saint – were treated with undue veneration, and thus had become idols. And they condemned the lewd chatter and bawdy behaviour in which pilgrims frequently indulged. The Roman Catholic countries had no such anxieties, but even there by the nineteenth century the old pilgrim routes were falling into disuse. In recent decades, however, a new spirit of pilgrimage has blown across the Western world. As people can take more weeks leave, increasing numbers spurn the bustling seaside resorts and the overcrowded historical sights, and instead travel to places of spiritual power: they may follow the steps of a great saint, such as Patrick of Ireland, to churches, monasteries and caves associated with his life; or they may visit ancient monasteries and abbeys. And having arrived at a monastery, they may stay a number of days and nights there in retreat, worshipping with the monks.

In addition to such traditional sites of pilgrimage, places of great natural beauty have also come to be regarded as sacred, to be visited in a spirit of veneration. In a world where human greed has destroyed so much of God's creation, we are drawn to those remaining areas where Nature is untrammelled – where God's handiwork can still be seen in all its awesome glory. And to their credit, governments throughout the world have begun to protect such areas, preventing timber and agricultural firms from chopping down the trees and ploughing up the land; and they have laid footpaths so people can enjoy the beauty without destroying it. Indeed the reverence and care with which these sites are now treated is reminiscent of the devotion which the medieval church showed towards saintly tombs and relics.

For the most part the modern pilgrims are individuals and families. But local churches now organize pilgrimages, in which a coach may take forty or fifty people to a place of holiness. In addition to the spiritual value of such trips, the church members experience the same blossoming of friendship as Chaucer's Canterbury pilgrims enjoyed. By seeing each other in a new context, by sharing the rigours of the journey, and by laughing, chatting

and even singing together, the invisible barriers of cautious pol-
iteness break down, so when they return home the life and
fellowship of their church is warmer and more trusting. Children
too can enjoy the relaxed atmosphere of a pilgrimage, feeling
themselves to be full members of the Christian community in a
way that is impossible within the formal context of Sunday
worship.

When it comes to festivals and the Sabbath, however, the
picture is far less happy, as secular forces overwhelm traditional
observance. In most Western countries Sunday has ceased to be
a time of worship and rest, becoming for most people a day of
frenetic pleasure-seeking and lucrative trading. And Christians
too are often swept along, missing church to share the fun and
the profit. Advent as a season of penance has almost disappeared,
and is now filled with parties and frenzied preparation for
Christmas; and the religious and moral meaning of Christmas
itself is now largely lost beneath the weight of food, alcohol
and inane television programmes. Lent still survives amongst
Christians as a period of abstinence, giving up one or two favourite foods, and of additional study; but Easter is often an awkward
anti-climax, the mysterious story of Christ's resurrection failing
to fire the modern Western imagination – because it does not
concur with modern Western rationality. The third great Christian festival of Pentecost now barely registers, especially in those
countries where the following Monday has ceased to be a public
holiday.

It is extremely difficult for Christians – or, indeed, people of
any other faith – to generate a festival atmosphere when the
society around them is indifferent. Christmas only survives as a
high point in the religious calendar because it is also a secular
celebration; so the Church can, as it were, borrow back from
the secular world a festival spirit. But, as the secular world
ignores the Sabbath and the other major festivals, Christian
celebrations are liable to feel flat. Yet Christian churches can
resist these trends if, as in a monastery, the whole community
gathers to celebrate together – and if, as in a monastery, people
have prepared for the festival with a period of penance. Through
eating simpler food, and through making our worship more

austere during Advent and Lent, we find ourselves turning inwards, reflecting on our own spiritual journey and confessing to God the times we have stumbled; thus when the festival finally arrives, our bodies are hungry for good food and our souls ready to receive God's blessing. Through coming together for some kind of feast as well as for worship, the physical pleasure of the meal and the spiritual peace of knowing God's forgiveness combine to create an atmosphere of uninhibited joy.

Such a festival becomes a true holiday – a holy day. Just as each day needs a regular rhythm of work, worship and rest, so too does each week and each year. This daily, weekly and annual rhythm is vital to our mental balance and physical well-being. Thus the Sabbath, the annual festivals, and the occasional pilgrimages help to make and keep us whole.

## TASK

Look back over the past twelve months, writing down the holidays you took, both single days off work and more prolonged periods. Ask whether you had enough time off, and whether you used that time well, to restore your vitality – or whether the holidays were as stressful and exhausting as work itself.

# MINISTRY

What brings joy to the heart is not the ministry which is given, but the love which inspires that ministry.

Aelred

# MINISTRY

Benedict in his rule expresses strong anxiety about ordained priests joining the monastery. He is worried that the other monks might treat them with deference, showing undue respect because of their office; and that the priests themselves might expect special privileges, such as better food and a higher place at table, and might refuse to undertake manual work, pronouncing it beneath their dignity. To Benedict any such division between clergy and laity would destroy the integrity and harmony of the community. Moreover he believed that every monk – indeed, every sincere Christian – is a priest in the sense of being used by God as a channel of divine grace to others.

Benedict's strictures about priests are echoed in the writings of every great monastic founder and reformer. Monasticism is at root a lay movement, with a strong egalitarian emphasis. This, however, left the monastic orders with the problem of creating a pattern and style of leadership which preserved equality and encouraged the sharing of ministry. Some monastic visionaries, such as St Francis, shunned any idea of hierarchy, preferring a glorious anarchy in which the Holy Spirit ruled directly through people's hearts. Unfortunately even within his own lifetime the order which he founded was already developing rigid structures which turned out to be both authoritarian and priest-ridden – although in subsequent generations many attempts have been made to reverse this. Benedict for his part had no doubt that a clear framework was needed, through which the Holy Spirit could guide the monastery. He thus required each monastery to elect an abbot, who, as the title implies, would act as father to the community. The Benedictine abbot has absolute power, within the moral limits of the Christian faith itself. But his task, according to Benedict, was not simply to issue orders which must be obeyed; rather, he should constantly listen to his monks, striving to discern the Spirit's guidance in their words, and thence articulate this guidance to the community. Unhappily Benedict's hierarchy proved no less prone to abuse than Francis's anarchy, so that by the medieval period many Benedictine abbots were little more than petty tyrants.

Going further back to the origins of monasticism, Pachomius instituted a most remarkable structure of leadership which gave the individual monks a high degree of freedom, yet maintained both social order and spiritual discipline. And it has stood the test of time, lasting in Ethiopia for sixteen centuries with remarkably little corruption. Within the Pachomian community there are two distinct types of leader: spiritual leaders and material leaders. The spiritual leaders, who tend to be older monks, act as spiritual directors and confessors to the monks, and are also concerned with discipline, deciding on the penance for any infringement of the monastic rule. They are chosen by the unanimous wish of the community; and they in turn appoint the material managers. These include the abbot and the other officers, who tend to be younger monks; and they are concerned exclusively with organizing the practical work of the monastery and managing its resources. In reaching practical decisions the abbot and his officers are required to consult the monks, listening carefully to their views; and if they begin to act tyrannically, they can, after due warning, be dismissed from office by the spiritual directors. For their part, the spiritual directors cannot become tyrants, since by virtue of their office they cannot make any practical decisions themselves – and, besides, they can be dismissed by the community.

So the abuse of power which has plagued Western monasticism is held firmly in check. More importantly, it is a system of leadership which enables everyone to play their full part in the life and ministry of the Community. Since the spiritual leaders have no direct power, and are hence not responsible for giving orders to people, they can concentrate on seeking to discern the talents, both practical and spiritual, of the monks under their guidance; and they can then encourage them to develop and exercise those talents. Moreover their close, intimate contact with the monks enables them to hear people's views and anxieties, and, if necessary, they can convey them to the practical leaders, to ensure they are taken into account.

As individuals we have only limited influence over the various organizations to which we belong – the firm where we work, the church we attend and so on. Yet a Pachomian division between 'spiritual' and practical leadership makes for good management, and is thus embedded in many managerial structures; so we for our part can help it to work well. Within Christian churches both the Anglican and Methodist churches have such a division in their traditional ministerial pattern: Anglicans have a priest in charge of spiritual ministry, and churchwardens with practical responsibility; Methodists have ordained ministers and stewards. In practice very often the priest or minister runs everything, with churchwardens or stewards acting as assistants – a tendency which may seem fair since the ordained clergy are usually paid, while the others are voluntary. As a result the spiritual gifts of the people are rarely harnessed. With insight and sensitivity we may find opportunities to boost the practical authority of churchwardens and stewards, and urge clergy to see themselves as spiritual directors, discerning and encouraging the talents of their flock.

In recent years, as the art of management has burgeoned into a major academic discipline, many writers have stressed the role of manager as 'facilitator'. Inefficient, weak managers tend to hold all power to themselves, unwilling to trust anyone else with real responsibility; as a result the gifts of those under their charge are wasted, while they themselves are struggling to do jobs for which they have neither the ability nor the time. The successful firm or workplace has senior managers who listen to their staff, and thence enable ideas to flow; and they see their prime function as drawing out the abilities of every member of staff, so they can be used to the best effect. Good managers thus make few practical decisions themselves, but decide who should make those decisions – thus emulating the role of spiritual director in a monastery.

In our small way we can each foster such enlightened ideas in our own church and workplace – and we may be surprised at how willingly they are accepted. But prior to trying to influence others, we must look to ourselves, asking whether our own potential for ministry is being fully realized. In the Pachomian monastery even the spiritual leaders, who guide and direct others, have spiritual leaders from whom they seek guidance for themselves. So we should each try to find someone who can be our spiritual guide. It may be a clergyman or a friend whose insight we respect; and we must ask that person to help discern our true gifts and talents – and also to tell us our limitations, so we do not foolishly attempt some ministry which is beyond our capacity.

Equally when we find ourselves in a position of leadership, we should beware of becoming autocratic, taking all authority to ourselves and issuing orders to others. We should remember that we are only worthy of our position insofar as we can listen to those in our charge, hearing and responding to their ideas, and discerning and developing their gifts. It is not a sign of weakness to be influenced by others, and to change your mind in the light of what they say; on the contrary weak people are stubborn, while those blessed by God with moral strength are happy to recognize the superior judgement of others. Nor is it a sign of weakness to entrust others with responsibility; on the contrary the greatest test of leadership is the ability to turn others into leaders.

## TASK

Think about someone you know well, and write down their gifts and talents, being as generous as possible in your assessment. Then do the same for yourself, being equally generous. Look at the list you have made of your own gifts and talents, and ask whether you are using them to the full.

# DEATH

Many a man in apparently good health, with blameless personal habits, has gone to bed without a care, but was not alive when morning came. So we must always be ready to die and thence to give an account of ourselves before our Maker.

Ignatius

# DEATH

When after a long eventful life the great Celtic monk Columba decided that his work on earth was complete, he began to pray that God would take him. Each evening he went to the chapel on Iona, and asked God to make him ready for death and then to receive him into heaven. Finally during Lent in 597 pains within his stomach convinced him that his hour was close; but he then asked God to delay his death until after Easter, so as not to spoil the monastery's celebrations. Once Easter was over, he asked a young monk to carry him round Iona. He first checked the barns, to assure himself that his brethren would have enough food until the next harvest. Then he went to each of the monastery animals, who knew instinctively that their beloved abbot was about to depart, and so hung their heads in sorrow. Once he had bid farewell to the horses, cattle and sheep, he told his brethren that he was about to die, so they could come to his cell in turn, to embrace him for the last time. Finally on the night of his death he received Communion in his cell, and afterwards managed to walk over to the chapel where he lay down and died in front of the altar.

There are innumerable similar accounts of the deaths of famous monks and nuns. And they describe how every monk and nun wishes to die – and how most succeed in doing. Many forms of daily monastic worship contain a prayer that one will be spared a sudden death, but rather have ample warning so that one can prepare to meet God. And since most monks and nuns have few fears of death, regarding it as the final and happiest stage of their spiritual journey, they readily recognize the early signs of terminal sickness. During the last months they can hand over their various responsibilities within the community to others, and devote themselves increasingly to prayer. In most monasteries a dying monk receives his brethren one by one in his cell, as Columba did, to ask forgiveness for any past wrongs and to bid farewell. And at death itself his confessor is by his side, to hand him in prayer to God.

Funerals too have a robust realism. Many monasteries preserve the medieval custom of wrapping the body in a cloth, or at most putting it in a flimsy box, rather than using a solid, heavy coffin. In this way it decomposes faster, so that in thirty or forty years the grave can be re-dug. And instead of permanent memorial stones, they have simple wooden crosses which will also disintegrate within a few decades. The funeral services themselves usually have a strange informality and intimacy, since the dead man was a close friend and spiritual brother to almost everyone present. His favourite hymns are sung, his favourite music played, and very often the address is peppered with affectionate anecdotes about him.

A prayer to be spared a sudden death was carried from the monastic worship into Cranmer's Litany, which was recited by generations of Anglicans until this century – when it has largely fallen into disuse. Today most people, when they allow themselves to contemplate death, express the desire to die suddenly, regarding death as a fearful event that should not cast a backward shadow over life. And funerals are often ambivalent, uneasy affairs in which large sums are expended to little purpose. The heavy oak coffin, lined in soft silk, is not so much a sign of respect for the departed loved one, as an attempt to pamper him – as if his body had not died. And the stone memorial is not only a comfort for the bereaved, but a further attempt to deny the physical finality of death by leaving a permanent mark on earth. Paradoxically the crematorium seeks the same deception by the opposite means: the clinical cleanliness of the crematorium chapel is reminiscent of a hospital where people are cured; and the dead body is whisked away, out of sight and out of mind. The modern way of death is spiritually and emotionally unsatisfactory – because we find it difficult to confront squarely the realities of death. As a consequence many bereaved people find it hard to grieve naturally and fully, and thus often take an extremely long time to re-emerge into the light of life – or can remain stuck at some early stage of grief.

The hospice movement, which in recent decades has begun to change our attitude to dying and death, was in part inspired by monastic wisdom. The founders, such as Cicely Saunders, wanted to turn the final months of life into a period of peace, love and joy. Medically their primary concern is the alleviation of pain, rather than artificially prolonging life. Spiritually they encourage people to face and embrace the prospect of imminent death.

As in a monastery, dying in a hospice is a very sociable affair. Patients are urged to invite family and friends to see them, in order to complete their relationships on earth. And there is always a counsellor – a secular confessor – available with whom the patient can share his innermost anxieties and fears, and thence receive comfort and reassurance. In many hospices pet animals are welcome also, since, like Columba, the patient needs to bid farewell to his animal friends.

As yet there are no signs of similar sanity being applied to funerals. Apart perhaps from choosing hymns, we make no preparations for our funeral before dying; so when death comes, the bereaved family has only a few days to arrange the funeral – giving them little choice but to follow the usual pattern, under the guidance of a professional funeral director. Moreover there are strict laws governing the disposal of human remains, in order to ensure hygiene, which further restrict our freedom. Yet as modern monastic practice illustrates, there is still considerable scope for improvement. When a loved one dies, we can ask the funeral director for the flimsiest coffin possible, without any expensive lining. And if the body is buried we can resist all pressure for a memorial stone, and have instead a simple wood cross on which the person's name is carved. There do not need to be professional pall-bearers at the service itself; we can revert to the old practice of friends and relatives carrying the coffin. And, if the local priest did not know the person well, the address should be given by a close friend or relative, who can recount anecdotes about the dead person to illustrate their personality – and thus create the warm intimacy of a monastery funeral. Even if the body is to be cremated, the service should take place in a church, both because the sacred beauty of an old church is more appropriate, and because the services can be as long as people want, with perhaps more than one person offering a tribute and with a number of favourite hymns.

It is sometimes said that the inept way in which modern Western society handles dying and death is due to the decline of religion: most people, it is asserted, no longer believe in life after death, and so regard death as an enemy to be avoided, rather than a friend to be welcomed. While there is undoubtedly some truth in this observation, close contact with monastic life suggests a rather different explanation. Monks who have devoted their whole lives to prayer rarely deal in theological certainties, but know that every aspect of existence, including death, is a mystery beyond our comprehension. Thus they entertain all the normal human doubts about life after death. The difference is that they acknowledge and express those doubts, feeling no shame in their own weakness of faith and lack of understanding. And once a doubt is honestly recognized – even the greatest doubt of all, concerning eternity – it no longer retains the same fearful grip on the human imagination. It can then be offered to God in prayer – and subsumed within faith.

## TASK

Recall the death of someone you knew well. Then spend half an hour sitting comfortably in a chair, imagine yourself dying as they did. Afterwards reflect on your feelings about your death.

# EPILOGUE

Religion, like every other sphere of human endeavour, is subject to long-term movements and short-term fashions. In the mid-eighteenth century the English-speaking world was shaken by the Evangelical revival, in which the individual was urged to make a direct personal commitment to Jesus, as master and saviour. A hundred years later the Tractarian movement re-asserted the importance of the sacraments and of colourful ritual in Christian worship, and re-awakened people to the ancient spiritual traditions of the Church.

In the twentieth century the dominant movement has been Charismatic, emphasizing the gifts or 'charisma' of all believers. In its mild form this has involved lay people playing a more active role in worship, leading prayers, reading the lesson and even preaching. In its passionate form, there has been an explosion of spiritual ministries, with some people speaking in tongues, some offering prophecies, some laying hands on the sick to heal them, and everyone feeling free to pray and speak as the Spirit prompts them.

At the death of John Henry Newman, one of the founders of the Tractarian movement, an obituary was published in which a leading churchman claimed that the entire life and worship of Protestant and Catholic churches alike had been transformed by Newman's influence. The same could be said of the influence of the Evangelical leaders and the Charismatic visionaries. Initially all three movements evoked strong opposition and seemed to divide Christians. But after one or two generations the essence of their ideas had permeated the whole Church. Thus, without necessarily realizing it, we are all Evangelicals, Tractarians and Charismatics.

Today as the turn of a new millennium approaches, we can

feel the first stirrings of a new movement, which in the fullness of time will prove equally influential. We could call it the 'Holiness Movement'. At the material level it is a response to the ecological disaster which our species has wrought on this fragile planet; holiness implies seeking to live simply, in harmony with the natural order. At the level of personal relationships it is a reaction against the competitive individualism that has corrupted Western culture in the past two centuries; holiness implies a high regard for faithful personal relationships, in which people seek to coop-erate, supporting one another in the journey of life. At the spiritual level it recognizes that the doctrines and institutions of traditional religion, while still having much to offer, are irrel-evant to the majority of people; there is, nonetheless, a profound yearning for direct personal communion with God, submitting the will of the individual to the divine will.

It is often observed that the political, social and moral climate of today is remarkably similar to that of the last decades of the Roman Empire. Then, as now, there was a sense of impending economic and ecological collapse, not least because bad farming had laid waste the vast plains of Europe and Africa which fed the Empire. Then, as now, family and personal relationships were breaking down in the towns and cities. Then, as now, the traditional religious institutions, including the Christian Church, were seen by many as self-serving and inward-looking. This was the context in which literally hundreds of thousands of men and women left their homes, trekked out in the deserts and forests, and created a new social and moral order – that of the monastery. And may of those that remained in the towns sought to practise a monastic way of life in their own home. The monks and nuns and their lay followers had no hesitation in saying that their most ardent desire was to be 'holy'.

We may still flinch from such a word for fear that it sounds unduly pious and self-righteous. But no monk ever pronounced himself as having achieved holiness; or if he did, he would thereby have tainted himself with the sin of pride! It is the aspiration to holiness that matters. And the ancient monk's desire for holiness is exactly the same as our own. Harmony with Nature is what the monks called poverty. Faithful personal relationship is what the monks called chastity. Submission to the divine will is what the monks called obedience.

# MONKS AND BOOKS

## AELRED (c. 1110–1167)

The son of a priest in Hexham, in northern England, Aelred as a young man worked at the court of King David of Scotland as steward of the royal household. He was naturally affectionate, but became increasingly disturbed by his own homosexual feelings. During a visit with King David to the new Cistercian abbey at Rievaulx, in Yorkshire, he decided to become a monk there – and never returned to Scotland. He eventually became abbot, and his gentle wisdom attracted visitors seeking his counsel from throughout Europe. His various books, of which the most beautiful are *Spiritual Friendship* and *Mirror of Charity*, extol the benefits of intimate friendship. They have recently been republished by Cistercian Publications, (Michigan, USA). And, with Pat Saunders, I have edited an anthology of his writings entitled *The Spiritual Kiss* (The Lamp Press, London 1989).

## ANTHONY (c. 251–356)

As a young man Anthony inherited a large estate in southern Egypt. But on hearing in church the story of Christ's encounter with the rich young man, he sold all his land and possessions, gave the money to the poor, and went into the desert to live as a hermit. For twenty years he remained in complete solitude, facing a series of spiritual battles with the devil. Then a monastic community formed around him, and he also began to travel widely, offering counsel and encouragement to churches, especially those suffering persecution. He earned the small amount of food he ate by making and selling mats. He is usually regarded as the founder of Christian monasticism. His life story was recounted by Athanasius, and various collections were made of his sayings. Numerous translations have been made, which can generally be found in anthologies of the lives and teachings of the 'desert fathers'. Athanasius's biography also appears in *The Fathers of the Primitive Church* edited by Herbert Musurillo (New York and London 1966).

## AUGUSTINE OF HIPPO (354–430)

The son of a pagan father and Christian mother, as a young man Augustine was attracted to the Manichee sect, which taught that bodily desires are evil and must be conquered by strict asceticism. But he found himself unable to adhere to their discipline, continuing to keep a mistress and enjoying good food and wine. In a state of acute guilt and self-hatred, he turned to Christianity, which previously he had despised as too crude and simple. He moved to Hippo in north Africa, near his native town, where he founded a monastery. And eight years later he became bishop. He was a brilliant theologian, and a doughty campaigner against those he regarded as heretics. But his monastic rule is remarkably practical and gentle. The rule was recently translated by Raymond Canning (London 1984).

## BASIL (c. 330–379)

Born of a distinguished and pious family, his grandmother, both his parents, and his two younger brothers were all acclaimed as saints. After his education in the finest universities of the eastern Empire, he became a hermit near Caesarea. But his reputation for wisdom spread so widely that after ten years he was pressed to become bishop of Caesarea. He founded numerous schools and hospitals, as well as setting up kitchens to provide food for the poor. He also took great care in seeking out the right men to be ordained as priests. There were numerous groups of monks in his diocese, and he composed a monastic rule to guide and

encourage them. He urged them to build guest-houses to receive
visitors, hospitals for the old and sick, and schools for the young.
His rule continues to be used throughout the Greek Orthodox
Church. A good collection of his writings can be found in *The
Fathers Speak* edited and translated by Georges A. Barrois (New
York 1986).


## BENEDICT (c.480–c.550)

If Basil is the patriarch of Eastern monasticism, Benedict enjoys
similar pre-eminence in the Western Church. After studying in
Rome, he went to Subiaco to live as a hermit. Soon others came
to join him, and a monastery was formed. But so acute was the
opposition to his leadership that an attempt was made on his life.
He moved to Monte Cassino near Naples where he established a
successful community, in which the monks lived in remarkable
peace. He composed a rule which displays great tolerance and
patience towards the frailties of human nature, as well as strict
spiritual devotion. Later Pope Gregory ordered that all monasteries in the western Church should adopt this rule, and it
continues to be followed by both the Benedictine and Cistercian
religious orders. There are many translations, including an excellent one by David Parry (London 1984).


## BERNARD (c. 1090–1153)

As a young man Bernard was renowned for his wit and elo-
quence, and seemed set for a successful career in politics. But at
the age of 22 he became a monk at the languishing and poverty-
stricken Benedictine community at Cîteaux. Under his influence
it was transformed, materially and spiritually, and a new
religious order was formed, known as the Cistercians, which
sought to return to the primitive simplicity of Benedict's first
monastery. He formed a new monastery at Clairvaux, and
monks from there in turn founded monasteries throughout
France and Britain – including Rievaulx in Yorkshire where

Aelred became abbot. As well as proving remarkably adept in financial and administrative affairs, he encouraged his monks in the way of mystical prayer. There are numerous translations of his sermons, letters and treatises, including a collection in the series 'Classics of Western Spirituality' (New York 1987).


## BRIGID (d 525)

As a girl Brigid defied the cruel and immoral ways of her father, who was a pagan chieftain. Finally her father sold her as a slave. She learnt the rudiments of Christianity from a fellow-slave, and decided to form a Christian community. Its site was under a huge oak tree, from which it derived its name, Kildare, meaning 'Cell of the Oak'. She and her fellow-nuns soon became famous for their generous hospitality to the poor and sick.


## CATHERINE (1347–1380)

The youngest of the numerous children of a dyer in Siena, Catherine at the age of twelve took a vow to devote herself entirely to Christ, whom she described as 'the sweet bridegroom of my soul'. By the age of twenty she was gathering a group of disciples, whom she spoke of as her 'family', to work amongst the sick and destitute. But she became increasingly conscious of her vocation as a teacher and counsellor. In 1370 she wrote the first of a series of public letters, on both spiritual and political affairs. And she travelled widely, urging individuals to repent and give themselves totally to Christ, and urging the Church to reform itself of its corrupt and worldly habits.


## CLARE (1194–1253)

A native of Assisi, Clare came under the influence of Francis at the age of eighteen, when she heard him preach. Following his example, she gave up all her worldly possessions. But as a woman

she was unable to imitate his wandering life. So Francis found
a small house for her in Assisi, where soon other young women
came to join her. Clare's community practised extreme poverty
and austerity, devoting themselves to prayer and contemplation.
Francis remained their guide, and they adopted his rule.

## DAVID (d. 601)

According to legend, David was born as a consequence of his
mother Non being raped by a Welsh chieftain. After being
educated at the famous school of St Iltut, he founded a monastery in the south-western tip of Wales. From there he and his
brethren travelled throughout western Wales, preaching the
Gospel and founding churches. He composed a simple rule
which is the only such document to survive from the numerous
Celtic monasteries of Britain and Ireland. An English translation
appears in *Celtic Fire* which I edited (London 1990, New York
1991).

## FRANCIS (1181–1226)

The son of a wealthy cloth-merchant of Assisi, Francis as a
young man was handsome and witty, enjoying the social life of
his native town. After a brief period as a soldier, Francis heard
a voice which seemed to come from the crucifix of a derelict
church, asking him to 'repair my house.' Francis renounced his
inheritance, and lived in the church, repairing its fabric with his
own hands. He then began travelling from place to place, preaching the Gospel and depending entirely on people's generosity.
Soon other men joined him, and the Franciscan religious order
was formed. His gentle charm and his love of Nature have made
him the most popular of all Christian saints. His rule itself is a
dull and pedestrian document, probably much influenced by his
advisers who were keen to gain the Pope's approval. But his
other writings, recently collected in the series 'Classics of Western Spirituality' (New York 1982) remain wonderfully fresh.

## IGNATIUS (1491–1556)

Like Francis, Ignatius was a rich and popular young man, enjoying good food and wine; and he was also briefly a soldier. But after a severe wound in battle, which left him with an awkward limp, he became a devoted Christian. And he decided to apply the courage and the discipline of army life to the service of Christ. He composed the Spiritual Exercises which are in effect a rigorous spiritual training course. And he formed the Society of Jesus, more commonly known as the Jesuits, to carry the Gospel to the remotest corners of the globe. The influence of the Jesuits on the religion and culture of every continent has been huge. And Ignatius's teachings, recently collected in the series 'Classics of Western Spirituality (New York 1991), remain a stirring call to spiritual battle.

## PACHOMIUS (d. 346)

If Anthony was the founder of Christian monasticism, Pachomius first formed monks into ordered communities, with a strict rule and pattern of life. Born in southern Egypt, he became a Christian when, as a soldier, he was deeply impressed by the kindness of Christians to those who were wounded or captured in battle. He initially lived as a hermit, but then in 320 formed the first of nine monastic communities. These were like large villages, with the monks producing all their own food and clothing, as well as looking after the poor and sick who came to them. He wrote the first monastic rule, and also insisted that the monastery leaders kept a strict account and diary of their community's activities, to ensure the rule was kept. The rule is still followed in the monasteries of Ethiopia. E. A. W. Budge's translation can be found in *The Paradise of the Holy Fathers* (New York 1909).

PHILIP NERI (1515–1595)

After working briefly in his uncle's business in Florence, Philip Neri travelled to Rome to study theology. He lived in a tiny attic, and earned a meagre wage as tutor to his landlord's sons. He spent his spare time in the streets and cafés of the city talking to young men about the Gospel. He won many converts, and was eventually ordained a priest. He formed a small community of priests who followed a simple rule of prayer and financial stewardship, without either taking vows or renouncing their property. He and his brethren continued to spread the Gospel in the streets of Rome, as well as welcome hundreds of visitors. Sadly there are no collections of his works available in English but there exists an excellent contemporary biography translated last century by F. W. Faber.

TERESA (1515–1582)

Teresa entered a Carmelite convent in her native town of Avila at the age of twenty. But it was not until the age of forty, when she experienced her 'second conversion', that she turned to mystical prayer. She had intense visions and raptures, in which Christ seemed to pierce her heart with a spear. In 1562 she founded a new convent, in which she and her followers adopted the primitive simplicity of the original Carmelites, including walking barefoot. She combined fervent prayer with robust common sense, and so proved both a great teacher and a formidable manager. By the time of her death she had founded a further sixteen Carmelite convents, following the primitive rule.